EBURY PRESS

AYURVEDA

Dr G.G. Gangadharan has been a champion of Ayurveda for the past three and a half decades. He is the author of ten research papers, twelve research articles, thirteen primary papers and six books. As a renowned expert on lifestyle diseases, he has conducted training programmes in the US, the UK, Germany, France, China, South Africa, Kenya, Nepal, Italy and Hong Kong, in addition to India. During his career, he has collaborated with social and corporate organizations, government think tanks, and international agencies that are interested in improving healthcare. After his seven-and-a-half-year Ayurvedacharya course from Coimbatore, Tamil Nadu, he acquired a master's degree from McGill University in Montreal, Canada. He is the recipient of the prestigious Ashoka Innovators for the Public fellowship. He also has a PhD from Tilak Maharashtra Vidyapeeth, Pune, in management of rheumatoid arthritis.

ADVANCE PRAISE

'Health and happiness are interconnected. Happiness is accomplished with good health. Ayurveda is a science of life that advocates the art of living happily and holistically, guiding us towards wellness in all dimensions of the physical, mental and spiritual sphere to become better people. Dr Gangadharan has commingled this fact and come up with an intriguing treatise in the form of this book'—Vaidya Rajesh Kotecha, secretary, Ministry of AYUSH

'*Ayurveda* by Dr G.G. Gangadharan is a refreshingly new take on the oldest medical tradition in the world. It strikingly illustrates the contemporary relevance of Ayurveda at a time when the world is fighting an unprecedented war against a global pandemic while undergoing an epidemiological transition towards multifactorial morbidity. As a scientist, I have been inspired and fascinated by the sophistication and depth of Ayurvedic concepts, such as *doṣa*, *rasayana* and *agni*. I believe this book will invoke similar interest and inquisitiveness among readers to know more about health, healing and wellness. The book, written in lucid language, may be of interest to a wide range of readers, including scientists, students and homemakers, as well as those seeking simple health tips and knowledge on this ancient science of healing'—Dr Bhushan Patwardhan, national research professor, Ministry of AYUSH, and former vice chairman of the University Grants Commission, New Delhi

'Creating a beginner's guide to essential scientific Ayurveda practices is a great idea. Dr G.G. Gangadharan's idea to look at the human body as an intelligent system reflects his out-of-the-box thinking regarding health, where happiness comes eventually. With a legacy of 5000 years, Ayurveda has always been a defender of our well-being. And today, to help the body keep up with a fast-paced world, we certainly need a time-tested defender rather than an experimental one. This book will certainly introduce you to this time-tested defender, Ayurveda'—Vaidya Jayant Deopujari, chairman, board of governors, Central Council of Indian Medicine, Ministry of AYUSH; guru, Rashtriya Ayurveda Vidyapeeth (National Academy of Ayurveda), New Delhi

AYURVEDA

The True Way to Restore Your Health and Happiness

Dr G.G. Gangadharan

Foreword by M.S. Valiathan, national research professor

EBURY PRESS
An imprint of Penguin Random House

EBURY PRESS

USA | Canada | UK | Ireland | Australia
New Zealand | India | South Africa | China

Ebury Press is part of the Penguin Random House group of companies whose addresses can be found at global.penguinrandomhouse.com

Published by Penguin Random House India Pvt. Ltd
4th Floor, Capital Tower 1, MG Road,
Gurugram 122 002, Haryana, India

Penguin Random House India

First published in Ebury Press by Penguin Random House India 2021

10 9 8 7 6 5 4 3 2 1

The views and opinions expressed in this book are the author's own and the facts are as reported by him which have been verified to the extent possible, and the publishers are not in any way liable for the same.

ISBN 9780143451976

Typeset in Adobe Garamond Pro by Manipal Technologies Limited, Manipal
Printed at Thomson Press India Ltd, New Delhi

www.penguin.co.in

To

M.R. Jayaram, for his unwavering support and guidance in my endeavours, including this book. I could not have written this book without his constant advice and encouragement

Dr Jayaram-ji is a spiritual leader, dharmadhikari of the Kaiwara temples and the chairman of Gokula Education Foundation (GEF), which leads the Ramaiah Group of Institutions

My pranam to you, sir

Contents

Section II: Case Studies

Foreword

Dr Gangadharan is a reputed Ayurveda physician, scholar, author and researcher, and a renowned expert in lifestyle diseases. This volume, titled *Ayurveda*, is his attempt, based on long professional experience, to convey the message of Ayurveda to a global readership. This quintessential message is that the mission of Ayurveda goes beyond the remediation of illness and seeks true restoration of the physical, mental and spiritual well-being of individuals. He also points out that the restorative process of Ayurveda is always done in harmony with manifestations of nature in time, habitat, fauna and flora, and unceasing interactions between the individual and the environment.

A traditional Ayurveda physician trained in the rigorous programme at Coimbatore and reverential to Ayurveda, Dr Gangadharan is fully conversant with sciences relating to laboratory and clinical medicine. His discussions in this book testify to his deep understanding of Ayurveda and Western medicine, and their increasing interaction since the advent of colonial rule in India. He has covered an astonishing range of subjects—ancient and modern, philosophical and scientific, conceptual and practical. He has drawn the attention of readers to many instances where the ancient insights of Ayurveda have found resonance in contemporary studies published in top scientific journals.

Consider the following examples:

***Doṣa prakṛti* and the human genome:** An individual has a constitutional type (prakṛti) fixed at conception. It has great importance because, among other things, it determines the individual's response to the treatment. In a multicentric study, of which Dr Gangadharan was a participant, it was shown that the prakṛti classification of individuals has a genomic basis. This would suggest that prakṛti-based determination of the human phenotype had anticipated the principle of pharmacogenomics many centuries ago.

Epigenetics: Epigenetics studies the distribution over the DNA chain of control molecules called methyl groups. They can attach themselves to the DNA chain and control the manufacture of proteins and what type of cell is produced. DNA methylation and changes brought about thereby are known to produce phenotypic variations and diseases. A multicentric study showed DNA methylation differences in the *vāta*, *pitta* and kapha phenotypes.

Additionally, there are interesting discussions on the Ayurvedic concept of the stages of incubation of a disease, gut and microbiome, and a ten-point-based diagnosis of diseases. The author has included several illustrative examples of the use of this method for making bedside diagnosis. According to

Professor Kutumbiah, this method excelled in making a diagnosis among ancient systems of medicine, including Greek.

Dr Gangadharan has shown rare candour in outlining the shortcomings of Ayurveda, such as the total neglect of Ayurveda manuscripts, inadequate effort for the conservation of medicinal plants, lack of standardization of products and processes, and the menace of the industry—the physician complex. There are also threats posed by fake physicians, fake medicines and fake institutions. Those who share the wish and power to put the Ayurvedic house in order will find it rewarding to study these observations of an experienced physician.

The value of the book is enhanced by the author's vision of 'summative medicine', which combines the best of different systems of medicine and is almost utopian. The glossary will be a boon to the uninitiated.

I have no doubt that this book, by an authority in Ayurveda, will be welcomed not only by Ayurveda students and physicians but also by those who are friends of Ayurveda.

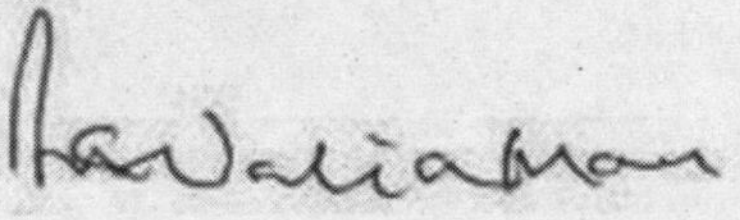

M.S. VALIATHAN
National Research Professor
(Padmabhushan Awardee by Govt of India)
9 May 2018

1

Introduction

There is no such thing as alternative medicine. If a treatment heals the patient, it is medicinal. If it doesn't, it is quackery.

The first thing you need to know about this book is that it is not a defence of Ayurveda. A sound, scientific framework of healthcare that has saved countless lives over 5,000 years does not need defenders. It needs champions. It needs to be given wings so that it can reach out to 7.5 billion human beings, most of whom are struggling to avail cost-effective and quality healthcare. This book was born because the world needs it. It is time for the human species to sit up and notice the unique blessings offered by Ayurveda.

The top-level unique boon of Ayurveda is the implicit promise of true restoration. The promise that the body and mind can be restored to the healthy state from which it descended into sickness. Instead of just managing the disease, Ayurveda invites the body–mind to regain its former glory. And no, this is not mythical, like the elixir of youth—it is based on holism, the idea that healthcare must address the individual as a whole instead of focusing on just the disease.

Every chapter in this book reinforces Ayurveda's founding principle of true restoration.

In the second chapter, 'The Whole Plant, the Whole Person', we will learn the benefits of trusting nature's design. When we use a substance wholly—the way nature designed—we do away with any potential side-effects that a synthesized variation could harbour. Everything we find in nature is potentially medicinal or potentially poisonous, depending on the method and the quantity in which we use it. And since one person's medicine may be another's poison, the first step in treating an individual is to ascertain how this individual is unique, so that the approach can be customized. As you can imagine, the benefit of curing the whole human using the whole plant is true restoration.

In the third chapter, 'Pathogenesis and the Path of Moderation', we get introduced to the six stages of a disease and how Ayurveda has the ability to detect it at the earliest stage. This gives us the chance to truly restore the body–mind in the quickest possible time.

In the fourth chapter, 'Prakṛti and the Genome', we talk about the three doṣas—vāta, pitta and kapha—which together determine the prakṛti, or intrinsic nature, of the individual. We talk about a scientific paper published in *Nature*, which maps unique genes to each of the doṣas. Ayurveda's knowledge of how the three doṣas work is integral to its promise of true restoration.

In the fifth chapter, 'Gut, GIT and Microbiome', we look at our digestive tract as an intelligent system capable of keeping most diseases at bay. The gut is home to countless bacteria called gut flora that help retain health. That is why Ayurveda rejects the carpet-bombing approach—any medicine administered must eliminate only pathogens and not helpful micro-organisms. So, Ayurveda's gut-friendly approach allows it to go beyond disease management and become a truly restorative healthcare framework.

In the sixth chapter, 'Epigenetics', we explore the impact of lifestyle and the environment on health. And we learn how to diet; daily rituals and periodic cleansing practices can keep the body–mind in prime condition—in other words, in a truly restorative state.

In the seventh chapter, 'Pillars of Restoration', we extend the learning gleaned from 'Epigenetics'. We understand, among other things, the impact of modern consumption habits, and how this impact can be managed. Again, it's all about restoration and health.

In the eighth chapter, 'Tailor-Made Healthcare', we understand how Ayurveda uses the profile of the individual—what makes the person unique—to customize medicines and treatment procedures. Ten factors go into a person's profile and each has a say in the medicines and procedures administered. Ayurveda has been doing for millennia what modern medicine has now begun to do with the advent of pharmacogenomics.

In the ninth chapter, 'Limitations of Ayurveda', we look at the reasons behind Ayurveda's limited influence on the global healthcare map. If we are honest, we must acknowledge why a truly restorative healthcare framework has neither the reach nor the respect it deserves.

In the tenth chapter, 'The Summative Approach', case studies and concepts explain how Ayurveda can be combined with modern medicine to offer the best care to almost anybody. Allopathy, a system that guarantees efficacy and immediacy, need not be at loggerheads with Ayurveda. When the two come together, both short-term demands and long-term needs of the individual can be fulfilled.

In the concluding chapter, 'The Future', we look at measures that can be undertaken to bring the restorative power of Ayurveda to the world.

After this, you will be able to read case studies that highlight the uniqueness and efficacy of Ayurveda treatments.

The twenty-first century belongs to non-communicable diseases, which are multicausal in nature. Lifestyle, diet, mental wellness and our genetic predispositions together attack us in a modern setting steeped in stress. With so many factors at play, we can no longer even pretend to come up with magic-pill solutions. Our healthcare must now offer sustainable and intelligent solutions. That's Ayurveda in a nutshell. Perhaps the twenty-first century will belong to Ayurveda.

Why Did You Pick Up This Book?

You may belong to one of the following categories:

- *You are a cynic:* You are convinced Ayurveda does not work and you'd like to snigger at a new rendition of its theories. Thank you for giving this book an oblique chance—and prepare to be surprised. This book will offer details and case studies that will make you want to rethink your opinions.
- *You are a sceptic:* You've come to the right place. You are looking for evidence and if you find it sufficiently, you'd like to qualitatively understand the framework. I promise you that your logical thinking will be satisfied and you will be left with a keen desire to learn more about Ayurveda.
- *You are just curious:* Thank you for your open-mindedness. Your curiosity is going to reward you. You will probably

finish reading this book with a huge question: How has the importance of Ayurveda been overlooked for so long?

- *You are a fan:* You already know Ayurveda works. Now you might learn why and how it works. Maybe this book will convince you to take another step and become a champion of Ayurveda. We need people to talk about Ayurveda—knowledgeably and clearly—hopefully from the largest and loudest podiums available. I hope you will read this book and gift it to people who could use it to further Ayurveda.

Who Am I?

Maybe you'd like to know a little bit about me—and understand the approach to my pursuit and its three dimensions. If not, you may skip to the next segment.

Collecting the dots

I have been working in the field of Ayurveda for over thirty years. My work has taken me all over India. During the early stages of my career, I was part of the Lok Swasthya Parampara Samvardhan Samiti (LSPSS), where our objective was to preserve local healing traditions. This involved travelling to different parts of the country, meeting local healers, documenting parts of their work and bringing them together through conferences and publications. My understanding of Ayurveda and local healing traditions grew manifold during this period.

As a result of this responsibility, I witnessed some extraordinary methods in practice across India and some proved to be real eye-openers.

In Rajasthan, I visited a healer of dental problems. Her village was situated in a far corner of the state, with only a few buses connecting it to the rest of the world. The healer lived in a hut with a small child. She appeared to be a widow. She had not received any formal education. On the afternoon that I had visited her, a woman with severe toothache had come to her for help. The swelling on her right jaw was visible and I remember she was in immense pain. The healer went out, plucked leaves off a nearby shrub, squashed them, extracted the juice and added a few drops of it into the woman's left ear. After a few minutes, she asked the woman to spit it out. I noticed there were plenty of wriggling worms in her spit. The swelling subsided miraculously and she felt her pain disappear. After profusely thanking her and giving her a small fee, the patient left.

This other time, I was visiting a tribal village deep in the heart of Maharashtra. The tribal chief served me dinner in his kitchen. In the middle of our conversation, I couldn't resist asking him about a weird object I had noticed hanging above the cooking fire. It was only because I was a doctor and he knew my background that he was willing to tell me what it was: the neck of a tortoise hung out to dry so that it could be used for medicinal purposes. Apparently, the tribals ate tortoise meat. He went on to explain that a tortoise's neck muscles are incredibly strong and controlled only by the will of the tortoise. Once the tortoise pulls its neck inside its shell, it is very difficult to pull it forward. This unique property was often utilized by the tribe for medicinal purposes. For instance, if someone was suffering from a prolapsed rectum or uterus—where the rectum or the uterus comes out of its place and sticks out of the body—he is treated with medicine made of the tortoise's neck. The dried neck is burnt inside a clay-covered pot and turned into a powder (black *mashi*). It is applied to the prolapsed organ and pushed inside. This process ensures that the organ stays in place. Weird as the idea sounds now, the tribe had been using it for centuries with demonstrable results.

In my fifteen years of working with LSPSS, I have traversed all parts of India, including the remote corners of the North-East, which has allowed me to stumble upon many local healing techniques. I have met people skilled in treating cattle and other animals. They have also designed a comprehensive system of care for snakebites.

I was fortunate to have spent years learning of these healing techniques and understanding how self-sufficient they were. In the long run, these experiences enhanced my understanding of the human body and medicinal treatments for it.

Collating the dots

Knowledge and inspiration kept finding me in unusual forms. While still part of LSPSS, I was told that an elderly scholar was interested in meeting me. I was intrigued and decided to pay him a visit. He was at least seventy-five years old and his health was deteriorating. He greeted me in tears. He had dedicated his life working on Ayurveda manuscripts and slokas (verses). For over fifty years, he had travelled across Kerala and some parts of Karnataka in search of old manuscripts. He had studied them, gleaned nearly 1,000 ideas that were useful and practical, practised them, translated them and preserved them. And now, at the end of his life, there was no one willing to read or publish his labour of love. He asked me if I could help him. I said yes, even though I did not have the funds for it.

I discussed the project with my helpful seniors at LSPSS and soon started working on it. But around the time the work was half done, the LSPSS was dissolved. To my utter dismay, I was informed that this project could no longer be supported. I fought long and hard to get funds from elsewhere. Eventually, the book was published and contained the practical wisdom of Ayurveda spread over 1016 A4-size pages. Even today, I use the book as a reference while treating people.

This experience also shaped me into a collator of healthcare ideas.

Connecting the dots

As a practising doctor and researcher, I have a keen interest in connecting the dots between Ayurveda and other sciences. This started when, as a student, I noticed the similarity between homeostasis and *tridoṣa* balance. Modern medicine stumbled upon the idea of homeostasis in the late 1800s. Claude Bernard was the first to notice the existence of an internal environment and called it milieu interieur. In the early 1900s, this concept was explored deeper by Walter Cannon and it was he who gave it the name 'homeostasis'. Ayurveda has been discussing the internal environment for thousands of years. Ayurveda's attempt to restore the doṣa imbalance of the body is, in principle, very similar to homeostasis.

I realized that there was merit in explaining Ayurveda's concepts using allopathic ones. This book is one of the grandest projects I've undertaken to connect the dots.

Ayurveda Myths

You are about to embark upon a journey of knowledge. The first thing to do is jettison myths and misconceptions. In my conversations with those unfamiliar with Ayurveda, I have realized that they carry at least one of the myths mentioned below.

Ayurveda Is Unscientific

As mentioned before, *Nature* published a paper in 2015 that I co-authored. It was titled 'Prakṛti' and was about how the genome-wide analysis correlates with Ayurveda; it established the scientific validity of the concept of prakṛti. For decades, many Western cynics scoffed at prakṛti as an unscientific idea. In fact, they said that since prakṛti could not be proved as a valid idea and since Ayurveda began its investigation by determining the prakṛti of an individual, Ayurveda was nothing but pseudoscience. But in the chapter 'Prakṛti and the Genome', you will learn how each of the three doṣas (vāta, pitta and kapha) correlates to a number of unique genes.

Throughout this book, I will underscore the scientific validity of each idea presented. But more importantly, I will be honest about the limitations of Ayurveda. In the past few centuries, Western medicine has leveraged scientific progress to make seminal breakthroughs. Ayurveda hasn't done the same. Yet, simply because it is still playing catch-up doesn't make it a non-science.

Ayurveda Is Static

Ayurveda has been evolving for millennia, but one must concede that the last significant addition to the science was made in the late nineteenth century. Back then, new plants were discovered and their medicinal qualities investigated. As a result, new treatment methodologies came into being.

The earliest texts, the Rig Veda and the Yajur Veda, mention only sixty plants. Till date, more than 1,200 plants have been used by Ayurveda. Even plants that came to India with the Europeans—plants such as tomato, tobacco and potato—were utilized as healing agents. These plants have been mentioned in the *Shaligrama Nighantu*, a text created in the nineteenth century.

Ayurveda Is Rigid

Today's Ayurveda practitioners leverage modern diagnostic tools to offer the best care possible to their patients. They can read a CT scan, a blood report or an EEG chart with as much proficiency as an allopath. Meanwhile, pharmaceutical companies that manufacture Ayurveda medicines rely on modern technology to deliver quality products.

While researching the prakṛti project, we used software developed by C-DAC, Pune, to determine the prakṛti of individuals. Like any science, Ayurveda has exhibited a willingness to adapt. This will become amply clear as you read this book, especially the chapter titled 'The Summative Approach'. The pioneering physician and surgeon Sushruta explicitly asks the practitioner to go above and beyond the science of Ayurveda and leverage newer scientific fields to become successful and productive.

Ayurveda Has Inferior Diagnostics

Just because Ayurveda acknowledges the efficacy of modern diagnostic tools doesn't mean it has inferior diagnostics.

In 'Pathogenesis and the Path of Moderation', you will learn how Ayurveda identifies the existence of disease at the earliest of stages.

In the chapter 'Tailor-Made Healthcare', you will be exposed to the sophisticated customization of treatment. This can happen only if the science can diagnose the unique condition of the individual's physical and mental state.

Ayurveda Is the Science of Brahmins

Ayurveda does not originate from a particular caste or sect. The first Ayurveda guru, Charaka, was a wanderer with a caste-free identity. Sushruta was born a Kshatriya. He was, in fact, the son of a king. Meanwhile, Vagbhata, the author of numerous classical Ayurveda texts, is believed to have been a Buddhist. Few visionary gurus of Ayurveda were Brahmins.

It is generally observed that people from scheduled castes and scheduled tribes are great practitioners of the science of Ayurveda. In Kerala, Ayurveda still thrives in some of the scheduled castes and tribal communities. In fact, when the Dutch governor Hendrik van Rheede was working on his book *Hortus Malabaricus*, he took help from an Ezhava (a 'backward' caste) physician Itty Achudan Vaidyan.

Ashtavaidya *parampara* is a Brahmin lineage in Ayurveda. But it's easy to see why the modern interpreter would equate Ayurveda with Brahminism. Both use Sanskrit slokas to preserve and propagate ideas. That shouldn't be surprising—back then, Sanskrit was the language of science as well as the language on the streets. Having said that, many ancient Ayurveda texts we use till date were created in other Indian languages. Again, that is quite logical—Ayurveda developed organically across the length and breadth of India. Over time, as other languages grew in influence, those languages were used to document brand-new solutions created within the framework of Ayurveda.

In short, Ayurveda has always been a people's science that does not discriminate on the basis of caste or any other divisive entity.

Ayurveda Is All about Herbs and Vegetarianism

Ayurveda promotes moderation instead of any form of extremism. While the bulk of Ayurveda medicines are plant-based, animal-based medicines are also used as needed. Many wonderful Ayurveda medicines have animal products in them, although vegetarian alternatives exist for most.

One way in which Ayurveda promotes moderation is by asking the individual to balance the needs of life and the afterlife. One can enjoy life while doing deeds to enjoy the afterlife.

Joy can be derived by consuming fruits and vegetables that are most suitable for the season and person. Also, some specific foods have been identified as wholesome and worthy of consumption:

- White pumpkin is the best creeper vegetable.
- Dry grapes are the best fruits.
- Green gram is the best among pulses.
- Red rice is the best among grains.
- Chicken flesh has optimal strength-giving qualities.
- Mutton soup (*māṁsa rasa*) offers the best nutrition and is digested easily during an illness such as influenza and tuberculosis (TB). For broken bones, soup of a mutton leg is great medicine.

Ayurveda neither promotes vegetarianism, nor embraces the consumption of meat with gusto. It respects individual choice and propagates a moderate path. Also, if a person is used to consuming meats (as part of one's natural diet, or *sātmya*), it will not advocate an overnight relinquishing of such a diet. Ayurveda also suggests that an individual's diet be aligned with lifestyle and profession. Those who do a lot of physical labour are better suited to the consumption of more meat.

Details of how Ayurveda uses animal-based products are provided in the chapter 'Limitations of Ayurveda'.

A great number of Indians are vegetarians, but as a civilization, India has meat consumers. Recent political developments might have stigmatized the consumption of some meats, but our ancestors knew better than to politicize science and medicine.

Ayurveda Treatments Are Inconvenient

Ayurveda treatments include oral medication, therapeutic tools such as massages, and lifestyle changes. Together, all of these help in sustaining health and restoring the body to its former glory.

Some of the oral medication might be bitter, but I believe taste should not be a criterion while choosing medicine. The good news is that many companies and institutions are finding ways to make these medicines more compact and palatable. Check out the chapter 'The Summative Approach' for more details.

Meanwhile, other treatment techniques—such as massages—can prove to be quite invigorating and relaxing for both the body and the mind.

Ayurveda Has No Equivalent of Antibiotics and Painkillers

Ayurveda offers equivalent medicines to the antibiotic and the painkiller. But the Ayurveda 'antibiotic' is intelligent enough to attack only pathogens and leave helpful gut flora undamaged. Similarly, the Ayurveda 'painkiller' does more than manage symptoms—it addresses the root cause while relieving pain.

Ayurveda Does Not Have Quick-Fixes

Ayurveda has a bevy of medicines designed to offer quick and permanent fixes for many diseases. Fever, for example, can be brought down quickly using medicines such as *amruthariṣṭa*, *sudarshana ghanavati* and *chukkamtippalyaadi vati*.

This myth stems from Ayurveda's promises of restoring health. True restoration can be an understandably time-consuming process that involves the expulsion of a lot of accumulated *aama* (toxins) from the body. However, if one follows the daily and seasonal rituals discussed in the chapter titled 'Epigenetics', restoring health need not be a lengthy process.

Ayurveda Is Just Another Disease-Management System

Ayurveda offers more than disease management. It offers total restoration—true healthcare.

Ayurveda treats not just the disease, but the complete person. The benefits of such an approach are discussed in detail in the chapter 'The Whole Plant, the Whole Person'.

After eliminating the immediate illness of the individual, Ayurveda shifts its focus to the prevention of disease and the promotion of health. This is a science that asks individuals to make the home a bastion of health, where the kitchen produces food that acts like medicine. More about this is discussed in the chapter 'Pillars of Restoration—Prevention and Promotion'.

Ayurveda Is Limited to India

Ayurveda believes that every geographical location is blessed with suitable resources to handle health concerns specific to that geography.

Researchers have discovered medicinal plants all over the world. Books have been written on medicinal plants available in Indonesia, Malaysia and Europe.

The spread and global relevance of Ayurveda has been discussed in the concluding chapter of the book. Understanding the science is important if one has to have this discussion.

Ayurveda Has No Cure for New Diseases

It is ridiculous to expect Ayurveda to have written down remedies for new diseases such as dengue and chikungunya. But thanks to timeless concepts, Ayurveda can treat such diseases effectively. After all, Ayurveda is all about addressing imbalances in the body, irrespective of how that imbalance was created in the first place. For instance, modern-day superbugs meet their match in Ayurveda's *pañca karma* treatment, which washes away all toxins and unhealthy organisms. This helps in the restoration of health.

Ayurveda Does Not Have Specializations

There are eight branches in Ayurveda:

- *Kaya*—General medicine
- *Bala*—Paediatrics
- *Graha*—Psychiatry and Psychology
- *Urdhwanga*—ENT and Eyes
- *Shalya*—Surgery
- *Damshtra*—Toxicology
- *Jara*—Geriatrics
- *Vrusha*—Sexology

Transitioning from Allopathy to Ayurveda Is Problematic

This book has many case studies and examples that debunk this myth. Not only can one move to Ayurveda, one can also avail a combination of Ayurveda and allopath solutions as needed. More details are available in the chapter 'The Summative Approach'.

Origin of Ayurveda in India

Perhaps it is helpful to ask the question: Why did Ayurveda originate in India? What factors helped it thrive in the subcontinent's civilization? There are, of course, some obvious social and cultural drivers. India was an advanced civilization that promoted the pursuit of knowledge and wisdom. As an intricate civilization, there was a dire need to find solutions to emerging problems—with healthcare demanding a chunk of the attention.

India is one of the twelve mega-biodiversity countries of the world. It has ten distinct biogeographic zones, which are further divided into twenty-five biogeographic provinces and over 426 biomes. The ten biogeographic zones in India are:

1. The Trans Himalayan
2. Himalayan
3. The Desert
4. Semi-arid
5. Western Ghats
6. The Deccan peninsula (including the Eastern Ghats)
7. The Gangetic plains
8. North-East India
9. Coasts
10. Islands

These ten distinct biogeographic zones are home to around 17,500 varieties of flowering plants. Of these, around 8000 have been used for medicinal purposes all over India by villagers, tribal communities and forest dwellers. As many as 1200 of them have been documented in ancient Ayurveda literature. Of these, 400–600 are commonly used and around a hundred have found incredible widespread use. In contrast, modern medicine makes medicines using no more than about thirty plants.

It's not surprising that Ayurveda, which relies on the supply of diverse plant—and animal—products, found a home in a biodiverse land.

Ayurveda also believes that every geographical location is blessed by nature with plants that are needed for the well-being of the community living in that area. Long before humans arrived on the scene, these plants adapted to epochal changes in the environment to become the most suitable life forms in that particular environment. So, they have intelligence that humans can tap into. For example, the Bushmen of Africa learnt to squeeze water out of hardy plants that dot the arid Kalahari desert. Those plants would not exist outside such a landscape. Similarly, the Gangetic plains and the Deccan peninsula have plants that will cure problems occurring in their respective geographies. Take the case of the ephedra plant, which is found at higher altitudes. Tea made of its leaves expands lung capacity—quite handy in a place with rarefied oxygen levels.

In the concluding chapter of the book, we will learn how to preserve this biodiversity and the subtle art of cohabitation on this planet.

Before Our Deep Dive

The first sloka of Ayurveda in *Ashtanga Hrudayam* reads:

Raagadi rogan satatanu shakthan
Asheshakaaya prasruthanasheshaan
Outsukhya mohaarathithanjaghana
Yo Apoorva vaidyaya namostu thasmai

—*Ashtanga Hrudayam Sutra Sthana, Chapter 1, Sloka 1*

The beauty of this sloka is that it starts with raga (mental aberrations) and not with *jwara* (fever) or any other physical manifestation. Ayurveda acknowledges that the mind is the most important organ in disease management. This sloka is a prayer to the Lord, the ultimate doctor, to keep us healthy, free from mental aberrations as well as physical diseases. It points out that everything is interconnected, from head to toe. And because our desires can be overwhelming, when we ask to be relieved of all diseases, we start with regulating our desires.

Another sloka of Ayurveda worth mentioning in the same breath reads:

Dharmartha kama mokshaanam
Aarogyam moolauttamam
Rogastasya apahartarah
Shreyaso jeevitasya cha

—*Charaka Samhita Sutra Sthana, Chapter 1*

This sloka is about enjoying life the right way. It asks the individual not to derail from the path of Dharma (principle). It says that for one to live with Dharma, *artha* (material sustenance), *kama* (desires and pleasures), and achieve moksha (salvation), *arogya* (health and harmony) is vital, for it is the foundation upon which all these are built.

Perform each act by following Dharma. Dharma is not a religious idea but a practical way of life. It is about aligning deeds with the role one is bestowed with—be it the role of a son, a father, a brother, a fighter, a doctor, a king or a butcher. Do the right deeds here, enjoy life the right way, and you shall enjoy the afterlife as well. Dharma, artha, kama and moksha are all important, but let's begin with Dharma.

These two foundational slokas of Ayurveda tell us why it is great science. Ayurveda cannot claim greatness because it is 5,000 years old. This longevity is merely a manifestation of its greatness. If the age of an idea proved greatness, greatness would have been found only in our museums. But Ayurveda belongs not in a museum but in the wider world. It is more relevant now than ever before. And I will spend the remainder of the book telling you why.

Section I

Concepts

2

The Whole Plant, the Whole Person

The plant that the West calls *Rauwolfia serpentina* is known in Ayurveda as '*sarpagandha*'. Ayurveda has been using it for centuries for the treatment of high blood pressure without any side-effects. Modern scientists have researched this plant and identified a master molecule named reserpine. They extracted it from the plant, synthesized it in a laboratory and used it to make medicines that would reduce blood pressure. The medicine achieved this objective, but also caused side-effects that included depression and suicidal tendencies.* After many fatal incidents, the medicine had to be retracted from the market.

There's a larger story behind this phenomenon—what I call the 'Sarpagandha Syndrome'. To understand this story, we need to know how nature works and how Ayurveda has moulded itself to fit into nature's contours.

* Douglas Lobay, '*Rauwolfia* in the Treatment of Hypertension', *Integrative Medicine*, June 2015, https://www.ncbi.nlm.nih.gov/pmc/articles/PMC4566472/

Nature, Wholeness and the Dynamic Equilibrium

We know that nature abhors a vacuum. Let's also acknowledge that nature abhors the lack of wholeness. At every point in time since the formation of our planet, every life form and substance found in nature has remained in a state of dynamic equilibrium—within itself and also with respect to its environment. If there is a momentary imbalance in that—for instance, if an unstable isotope is created—nature quickly restores the substance to its whole and natural state.

Meanwhile, nature uses chemistry to change biology over vast periods of time, so that every life form continuously evolves to a higher level of resilience.

Since nature sets such exacting standards for itself, is there any wonder that Ayurveda trusts it implicitly? By extension, Ayurveda trusts every plant and human body to be whole and complete. In the human body, this dynamic equilibrium is maintained by, among other phenomena, homeostasis; Claude Bernard, the father of experimental physiology, called this self-regulating ability the milieu interior. Since the human body and other natural life forms are designed this way, any imbalance in the human body—that manifests as a disease—can be addressed by using the restorative power of nature.

When we take a step back and look at the entire universe, we realize that nature is awe-inspiring. We realize that every life form is a microcosm of the entire universe. Since humans tend to be self-obsessed, let us rewrite that sentence as follows: The human body is a microcosm of the entire universe. The matter of the universe is in the human body and what is in the human body is in the universe. After all, astronomy tells us that the atoms that make up our body were produced inside a star. We share chemistry with the universe and, therefore, everything we find in it is potentially therapeutic for us.

So for the vaidya—the practitioner of Ayurveda—our planet is a boundless pharmacy. This makes the vaidya a bridge connecting the whole nature with the whole human being.

We will now look at how Ayurveda embraces the wholeness of the plant while also treating the human being in its entirety. In simpler terms, Ayurveda does not reduce a plant to its constituent bio-molecules. Nor does it reduce the human being to a set of ailing organs. Life is undoubtedly enabled by molecules and organs, but life is experienced in its entirety. Therefore, the processes that nurture and preserve life must be wholesome.

The first sign that Ayurveda is wholesome is the fact that its medicines do not cause side-effects if used appropriately.

No Side-Effects

Yes, Ayurvedic medicines cause no side-effects. The brazenness of this claim is made apparent by the fact that many allopathic medicines have a list of side-effects that's longer than the list of chemicals used to make them. Despite painstaking research that can last years—including clinical trials on various life forms and multiple iterations of development—allopathic medicines have been unable to shrug off the bane of unwanted externalities. Take antibiotics, for example—every generation of antibiotics is made stronger so as to vanquish newer generations of more resilient superbugs. This also means that every new generation of antibiotics takes a stronger toll on the human body, with the side-effects becoming starker. In such a dynamic domain, Ayurveda continues to use medicines free of side-effects, conceptualized and created many centuries ago. How has Ayurveda achieved this?

Well, Ayurveda studies plants in their entirety. Roots, stems, bark, flowers, fruits and leaves are understood—as constituent yet interconnected parts of the plant—and the therapeutic value of each part is understood. That done, Ayurveda identifies the best way to extract the plant's essence for human use.

Any part of any plant has hundreds of types of bio-molecules, such as alkaloids and saponins. In many cases, only one bio-molecule among these is capable of acting as the master molecule that combats the ailment. While allopathy will isolate, extract and synthesize this bio-molecule, Ayurveda will extract the entire part because it believes that the other bio-molecules in the plant negate the side-effects caused by just one of them.

This throws new light on the Sarpagandha Syndrome mentioned earlier. The plant sarpagandha behaves like a team, whereas reserpine behaves like the star player of that team, who is completely lost without his teammates.

The long and short of it is that Ayurveda trusts nature's design to be more holistic than its counterpart, the human design, and by embracing nature's holism, it manages to do away with potential side-effects.

Having said that, let's make another statement that, which at first glance, may appear contradictory: We don't take all parts of the plant or even everything within a single part of the plant.

All we are saying is that molecular-level selection of matter leads to problems. So, in Ayurveda, the vaidya removes those parts of the plant that are neither necessary for treatment, nor easily ingested by the human body. Through well-considered extraction methodologies, the physician makes the therapeutic qualities of the plant accessible to humans.

Extracting the Essence of a Plant

For a plant such as the holy basil, even the soil in which it grows is said to be medicinal. For other plants, we are interested in the therapeutic qualities of one or more of the following parts: roots, stems, bark, flowers, fruits and leaves. To infuse these qualities into a medicine, the raw materials need to be put through a predetermined extraction process.

Everything Can Also Be Potentially Harmful

Ayurveda demonstrates that if used appropriately, poison can work as ambrosia and, if used inappropriately, ambrosia can be as fatal as poison.

Ayurveda considers ghee, honey and gingelly oil (oil extracted from sesame seeds) master medicines that are extremely beneficial to the human body. A vāta prakṛti person, a pitta prakṛti person and a kapha prakṛti person can use gingelly oil, ghee and honey, respectively, as preferred carriers of medicine. Having said that, these very substances can cause imbalances in certain conditions:

- Overconsumption of ghee, having ghee at night and drinking cold water after consuming ghee are not healthy habits and can create blockages in arteries.
- Honey and ghee consumed in equal quantities can be poisonous. If these two have to be consumed together at all, one should be double the quantity of the other—else, we experience *mātrā viruddha* (dose incompatibility).

- Heating honey, pouring honey into hot drinks or consumption of honey by a person coming in from hot weather are all unhealthy practices. This is called *saṁskāra* viruddha (processing incompatibility). Drinking hot water after consuming honey is called *krama* viruddha (order incompatibility).
- Overconsumption of honey leads to constipation.

Now let's look at potential harmful impacts of other foods that are, on most occasions, healthy:

- Uncooked food and salads can be unhealthy in the monsoon. The same goes for pungent substances in the summer and cold substances in the winter. This is called *kāla* viruddha (time incompatibility).
- Daily consumption of large quantities of curd or consumption of curd at night is unhealthy. Boiled curds are especially toxic. Curds should be consumed with black pepper, moong dal (split green gram) soup or gooseberry pickle.
- Certain food combinations are unhealthy. Milk consumed with horse gram or fish causes *veerya* viruddha (potency incompatibility). Citrus fruit salad with milk is *samyoga* viruddha (combination incompatibility). The same goes for jackfruit and fish.
- Certain varieties of barley—an otherwise healthy food—can be toxic.
- Even water can be unhealthy—water from alkaline regions, for example. Meanwhile, it is already established that overconsumption of water puts extra stress on the kidneys, washes away important nutrients from the body and

> strains the system. Similarly, drinking non-boiled water can hinder the process of weight loss. Boiled water is light and easy to digest. It increases appetite and percolates well into the tissues. Cold water does not. Besides, drinking cold water immediately after having a hot beverage causes *parihar* viruddha (contraindication incompatibility). Hence, it is advised to boil drinking water.
>
> Meanwhile, cobra venom, an otherwise lethal substance, can save lives. Ayurveda uses medicines made using cobra venom for liver cirrhosis, cataract and chronic blocks.
>
> So the key question is not whether something is healthy or unhealthy. Instead, we can ask ourselves: Do we know enough about the intrinsic nature of the substance to understand when it will be healthy and when it will be harmful?

First, we need to remove fibre, starch and cellulose. You might wonder what else is left. Plenty! Medicinal plants are *veeryapradhana*, which means they are rich in secondary metabolites that form the base for medicines.

To make the plant material acceptable to and be assimilated by the body, we prepare pañca. These are five methods of extraction of the contents of a plant in dosage form, by which the body can assimilate it better.

Panca vidha kasaya kalpanas

1. *Kaṣāya* (decoction, or aqueous extraction)

The most commonly used extraction technique is aqueous extraction, where one portion of the herb is boiled with

X portions of water and boiled to reduce it to an nth portion of it. The proportion of water and the final concentration of the medicine vary based on the hardness of the raw materials. For instance, 4X water is added for soft herbs (herbs whose leaves and flowers are used), 8X water is added for medium hardness (including soft barks of plants, roots of shrubs and plants, soft roots, tubers and medium tubers) and 16X water is added where the plant material is too hard (including hardwood of trees, roots and root bark of trees and creepers).

The resultant decoction can be consumed as is or in different dosage forms.

When one wants to improve its shelf life and reduce its bulk considerably, one can further heat it to completely remove the water and keep it as a tablet. This is called ghanavati and cannot be used for secondary preparation such as *ariṣṭa, ghṛta, lehya* (these three have been explained as special dosage forms below), or as an ingredient in *basti* (enema).

2. *Svarasa* (juice)

Juice is usually extracted from a freshly collected herb—its leaves, fruit, stem or the whole plant. The juice is collected in a clean container and used immediately. Classical texts suggest methods to extract juice even from low-moisture herbs. The fresh juice of herbs is easily absorbed by the body and maximum effect is achieved in a comparatively short period.

3. *Kalka* (paste) or *Cūrṇa* (powder)

In this, either the fresh plant is used as a fresh paste after grinding it well or the raw material is dried under shade in a controlled environment and pounded to make powder. This dry powder can be used as such, internally, with or without adjuvant liquids, or it can be mixed with water to form a paste, which can be applied on the body.

4. *Hima* (cold infusion)

Hima is where herbs are soaked in cold water for a few hours or overnight for their essence to be extracted. These medicines usually address pitta problems.

5. *Phāṇṭa* (hot infusion)

Here, fresh or dry herbs in coarse powder form are put in hot water overnight to be filtered and used the next day. These medicines usually address kapha and vāta conditions.

All the above five basic preparations are used in other dosage forms, as explained below:

i) Alcohol extraction (*āsava/ariṣṭa*): Ayurveda has a unique preparation called āsava/ariṣṭa, when certain herbs are allowed to ferment in the base solution of jaggery and honey for a period of eight–ten weeks and, as a result, alcohol is formed. This alcohol extracts the medicinal essence of these herbs. No yeast or alcohol is added externally for the fermentation to happen.

ii) Oil or ghee preparation (ghrita or taila kalpana): Herbs are soaked or boiled in oil or ghee, and their essence is extracted by squeezing out the oil or the ghee.

iii) Lehya: Also known as *avaleha*, this is a semi-solid preparation obtained by boiling *swarasa*/kaṣāya of herbs, jaggery/sugar candy and ghee.

Needless to say, the correct extraction methodology for an input plant has been identified only after an in-depth understanding of the plant. Existing Ayurveda literature has listed out the optimal extraction methodology for hundreds of plants, and individual physicians do have the freedom to use some other methodology, provided they understand the *tattva* (intrinsic material nature) of the raw material. Otherwise, if an alcohol extraction is suggested, it is not to be replaced by a swarasa extract.

Ayurveda is also precise about the ingestion of the medicine, which can make use of the five sense organs, as well as all nine openings in the human body.

Having understood *why* we celebrate the holism of the plant and *how* we distil, it's time to understand how to treat the human being as a whole.

The Holistic Human

Even a casual observation of one's own body will teach one about referred pain. This is pain felt in one part of the body while, in reality, it exists in some other part. For instance, a person experiencing a myocardial infarction (commonly known as a heart attack) might experience pain only in the left jaw or the left arm.

Here are a couple of more banal examples of referred pain:

- An episode of indigestion or constipation leading to a headache in some people.
- Rapid consumption of really cold ice-cream leading to a 'brain freeze' moment—wherein nerves in the throat and palate transmit pain signals that feel like an ache in the head.

Referred pain is evidence, if at all evidence was needed, that all our body parts are interconnected. Ayurveda's power to truly restore the human body comes from worshipping this fact. That's why Ayurveda never treats an organ. It doesn't even treat the disease. It treats the human. Let's explain this by taking a common example.

Imagine a patient who has suffered a stroke and is suffering from oedema in his brain. In layman's terms, this means that there is now an excess accumulation of fluid in the brain. Ayurveda calls this condition *pakshaghata*. In it, the first step of Ayurvedic treatment is quite often treating the patient with unctuousness both internally and externally. This involves purgation and/or enema. The enema helps the patient excrete water from his body. The body, being a complete mechanism, understands surplus and deficit better than our politicians. So, through micro and macro channels that connect different parts of the body, additional fluid accumulation in the brain and other morbid elements are released by passing it to the intestine. The patient, therefore, recovers faster and, more often than not, regains control of his limbs.

For some allopathic specialists, the rectum (where the enema is administered) is a million miles away from the brain (where there is excess fluid accumulation). In Ayurveda, even though there are eight kinds of specialists, they are mandated to look at the person as an entity with specific needs at specific times.

The Uniqueness of the Holistic Human

Now, let's look at how we treat a patient holistically by acknowledging the uniqueness of their particular body.

Like allopathy, Ayurveda considers a patient's history to be crucial to the treatment process and diagnosis. In addition to the medical history of the patient, a vaidya will take into account other factors that make the case unique. So the following ten factors are studied to offer customized and holistic care:

1. ***Dūṣyas (Dhātus)*** are structural units of the body. The seven structural units are *rasa* (plasma), *rakta* (blood), *māṁsa* (muscle), *medās* (fat), *asthi* (bone), *majja* (marrow/nerve) and *shukra* (reproductive tissue).
2. ***Deśa*** has two parts to it—*deha deśam* (the body of the patient) and *bhoomi deśam* (the geography where the patient lives and, if relevant, where they were born). Depending on whether the patient lives in a marshland, a desert, a rainforest, etc., the treatment methodology can differ. So, for instance, medicine prescribed to a patient from the northern mountains of India can be different from the medicine prescribed to a patient from the plains in the south.
3. ***Bala*** alludes to the physical strength required to handle the medicines ingested into one's system. It is of three types: *sahaja bala* (by birth), *kālājā bala* (by season and age) and *yuktikruta bala* (by will or acquired using *rasāyanas*, which are fortified jam-like preparations that can rejuvenate body cells).
4. ***Kāla*** is also of two types: *roga* kāla, which is the current phase of the disease, and *kālanukrama*, which is the current climatic condition. In winter, you can prescribe stronger medicines, as the body's ability to digest is stronger then. In summer, medication has to be milder.

5. ***Anala*** is the digestive fire of the patient. Some patients may be able to digest the strongest and toughest medicines, while other patients may purge out the same medicine.
6. ***Prakṛti*** is the body constitution, perhaps the most important of the ten factors. Prakṛti classifies every patient as having a vāta, pitta or kapha constitution, or perhaps a combination of these. A medicine may be unsuitable for some constitutions while being suitable and reactive for other constitutions. If a hot-potency medicine is given to a person with a pitta prakṛti, he could end up with blisters all over the body and bleed through the rectum. But a kapha prakṛti person would feel the healing power of the same medicine.
7. ***Vaya*** means the age of the patient. Age is broadly categorized as *baalyam* (childhood), *yovvanam* (young adulthood), *madhyam* (middle age) and *vardhkyam* (old age). When one includes sub-categories, vaya has sixteen classified entities. Needless to say, one's ability to assimilate medicine changes with age.
8. ***Satva*** gives us a psychiatric assessment of the patient, more specifically, his emotional response to the illness. Some patients suffering from minor health issues may react to it like it's an emergency and seek plenty of attention. Some patients may be in acute pain and not show it. Ayurveda embraces a psychosomatic approach, in which both the body and the mind are addressed. Thus, a patient can be classified, depending on their threshold for adversity, as *pravara satva* (high threshold), *madhyama satva* (medium threshold) and *avara satva* (low threshold). A patient can be called '*satvavan*', where he is able to tolerate the disease and

able to withstand the treatment procedures and medications with strong mental fortitude.

9. ***Sātmya*** alludes to the general or personal habits of the patient. We usually allude to food, addictions and other lifestyle elements when describing sātmya (habituation) to a person. For someone who is addicted to alcohol consumption, stopping it at once could be fatal. Alcohol is sātmya to that person. Anything that is sātmya to a person and has wholesome effects should be continued. Otherwise, these habits should be gradually overcome.
10. ***Āhāra*** is the food an individual is accustomed to. Every individual has their unique patterns of food consumption that may or may not interfere with the treatment methodology. For someone from north India, wheat is sātmya. If ragi is prescribed to that person, they may find this hardy millet difficult to digest.

We shall study these ten factors in great detail in the chapter 'Tailor-Made Healthcare'. For now, let us remember the uniqueness accorded to a patient by these ten factors. It is the job of the vaidya to keep the patient's uniqueness in mind at all times so that personalized medication, care and support can be administered.

Only by understanding the whole plant and the whole human can a vaidya prescribe the most suitable medicines for each patient.

In Conclusion

The most popular therapy model in modern psychology is the non-directive, person-centric Rogerian approach, pioneered by Carl Rogers. Here, the therapist addresses the needs of the person instead of focusing on the problem faced by the person. This is quite similar to how Ayurveda has approached healthcare since time immemorial.

Ayurveda is way beyond disease management. It is a framework for life. That's self-evident, isn't it, considering that the literal translation of Ayurveda is the 'science of longevity'?

Ayurveda achieves this by understanding the whole plant and treating the whole person. The human body mirrors the interconnectedness found in nature. Nature has its own ways of correcting imbalances and it has taught these tricks to every life form, including human beings. When we know this, we begin to understand Ayurveda and its potential to offer true restoration.

3

Pathogenesis and the Path of Moderation

The word 'pathogenesis' alludes to the progression of a disease through various stages. Ayurveda has identified six distinct stages of a disease, and it goes without saying that the earlier a disease is identified, the easier and quicker it is to restore the body to its healthy state.

We shall explore the six stages of disease later in this chapter. For now, let's ask a more basic question: Why do we fall ill? The answer is imbalance, which can occur in one of two ways.

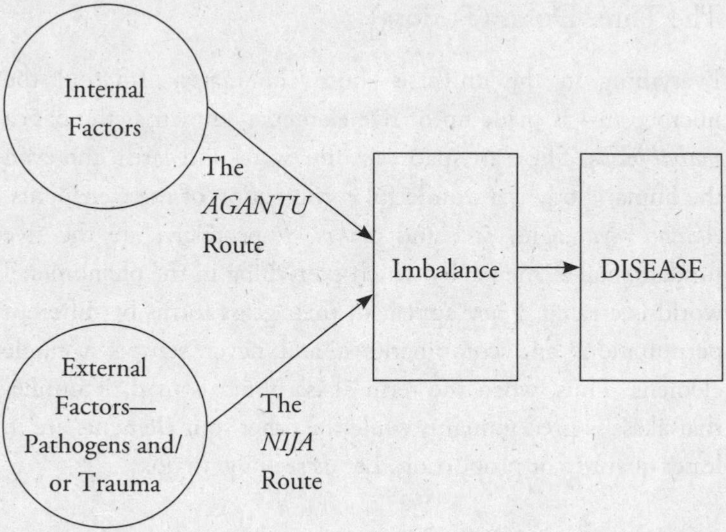

- The *NIJA* route: An imbalance is created inside the human body without any explicit external stimuli and also refers to unsustainable lifestyles, dietary patterns, medicine consumption, etc., that are within a patient's control, leading to intrinsic factor (doṣa, dūṣya) vitiation.
- The *ĀGANTU* route: An imbalance is created by the invasion of foreign microorganisms or by a trauma such as an external injury. It refers to traumatic/external causes not in the control of a person or that which unconsciously affects him/her—such as exposure to excess heat or food poisoning.

Once the imbalance is created, the disease progresses in exactly the same way, irrespective of how the imbalance got created.

Peeling the next layer of the pathogenesis onion, we ask: What causes the imbalance? To answer this question, we need to understand tridoṣa.

The Three Doṣas (Tridoṣa)

Everything in the universe—both the macrocośm and the microcosm—is made up of five elements, known as the pañca *mahābhūta*s. These are space, air, fire, water and earth, and even the human body is a wonderful combination of these elements. *Ākāśa*, *vāyu*, agni, *jala* and *pṛthvi,* respectively, are the five fundamental elements, by which everything in the phenomenal world is created. They appear in their gross forms by different permutations and combinations, and never stay as a single element. Thus, when the term ākāśa bhūta is used, it implies that ākāśa is predominant, while the other four elements are in lesser quantity or proportion. Let us see how that is:

1. *Ākāśa:* Esoterically speaking, we can link space with soul or spirit—that quintessential primal energy that keeps the body alive. Materially speaking, space can refer to the intermolecular spaces that exist in all matter. Ākāśa is associated with sound.
2. *Vāyu:* Respiration can be connected with the element of air—so it can relate to the creation of gases during digestion. Vāyu is associated with tactile sensations and sound.
3. *Agni:* Maintaining homeostasis (uniform body temperature), digesting food and other such functions are made possible by the element of fire. Fire has the qualities of sound, sensations and form.
4. *Jala:* Seventy per cent of our bodies is water—the fourth element. Jala has the qualities of sound, sensation, form and fluidic nature.
5. *Pṛthvi:* This is the solidity principle of the body—the gross body; it creates the forms we perceive. It has the qualities of movement, sound, sensations, form, fluidity and solidity.

The tridoṣa—vāta, pitta and kapha—are each made up of two of the five elements mentioned above.

Vāta = Air + Space

Manages motion: Principle of movement, including nerve conductions

Pitta = Fire + Water

Manages digestion and metabolism, including all biochemical changes in the body

Kapha = Earth + Water

Manages cumulation: Principles of cohesion—includes all solid particles in the body

These tridoṣa are present all over the body and they manage the functioning of the body. Hence, vāta, pitta and kapha are called the functional units of the body. As is evident from the diagram, vāta manages all movement in the body, including neural, vascular and cellular; pitta initiates and regulates all transformation in the body, including all levels of metabolism; and kapha represents cumulation, cohesion and tissue mass that create body structure.

When the tridoṣa do their assigned functions, the body stays healthy. When the doṣa are vitiated, they cause problems in the smooth functioning of the body. This is called doṣa imbalance.

Doṣa Imbalance

Each of the tridoṣa has five sub-doṣas, and each of these sub-doṣas has a specific place to reside in and specific functions to do. An illness begins when these doṣas move from their specified places or start to accumulate in one place.

Where these doṣas reside and what they do is explained well in Ayurveda.

Types of Vata

1. ***Prana Vata:*** Prana is located in the head; it moves in the chest and the throat. It regulates functions of the heart, the sense organs, the intellect and vision. It is the cause behind expectoration, sneezing, belching, inspiration and swallowing of food. It is considered the force that takes care of the functioning of the heart, the lungs and the throat.
2. ***Udana Vata:*** The chest is the seat of Udana; it moves in the nose, umbilicus and the throat. It is responsible for functions such as the initiation of speech, enthusiasm, strength, colour, complexion and memory. It is correlated with breath and the process of respiration.
3. ***Vyana Vata:*** Vyana is located in the heart and moves all over the body at great speed. It attends to functions such as flexion and extension (locomotor action), the opening and closing of the eyelids, etc. It is related to blood circulation and muscle activities.
4. ***Samana Vata:*** Samana vata is located near the digestive fire. It moves in the gastrointestinal tract, receives food into the stomach, aids in digestion, helps in dividing the food into useful and waste parts, and moves these parts in their normal paths. It is limited to the digestive tract, assisting in normal downward peristalsis.

5. ***Apana Vata:*** Apana vata is located in the large intestine; it moves in the waist, bladder and genitals. It attends to functions such as ejaculation, menstruation, defecation, urination and childbirth. It maintains all excretion processes related to the lower half of the trunk.

Types of Pitta

1. ***Pachaka Pitta:*** It is located between the large intestine and the stomach (between amashaya and pakvashaya). It is composed of all the five basic elements (panca mahābhūta). It is devoid of the water element. It aids in digestion and transformation of food, and divides it into essence and waste. It graces and influences the other types of pitta. Hence, among all the types of pitta, pachaka pitta is the dominant one.
2. ***Ranjaka Pitta:*** The pitta, located in the amashaya—stomach—is known as ranjaka. It converts the useful part of the digestion into blood.
3. ***Sadhaka Pitta:*** The pitta located in the hrudaya—heart—is known as sadhaka. It attends to mental functions such as knowledge, intelligence and self- consciousness, thereby helping the purpose of life.
4. ***Alochaka Pitta:*** It is located in the eyes. It helps in vision.
5. ***Bhrajaka Pitta:*** It resides in skin and helps in the exhibition of colour and complexion.

Types of Kapha

1. ***Avalambaka Kapha:*** It is located in the chest and at the meeting place of the shoulders, the neck and the back. It lubricates and nourishes—functions that are attributed

to the water element. It also influences the functioning of other types of kapha.

2. ***Kledaka Kapha:*** It is located in the stomach. It moistens the hard food mass and thus aids in digestion.
3. ***Bodhaka Kapha:*** It is located in the tongue. It helps in taste perception.
4. ***Tarpaka Kapha:*** It is located in the head. It nourishes the sense organs.
5. ***Shleshaka Kapha:*** It is located in the bone joints. It lubricates and strengthens the joints.

Triggers of Doṣa Imbalance

When each doṣa has such a specific place to be at and a specific job to do, what makes it move out of its assigned places and/or get accumulated in one place? The answer: improper usage of kāla (time/season), artha (sensory objects) and karma (deeds).

In fact, the diagram explaining the manifestation of a disease can be redrawn as follows:

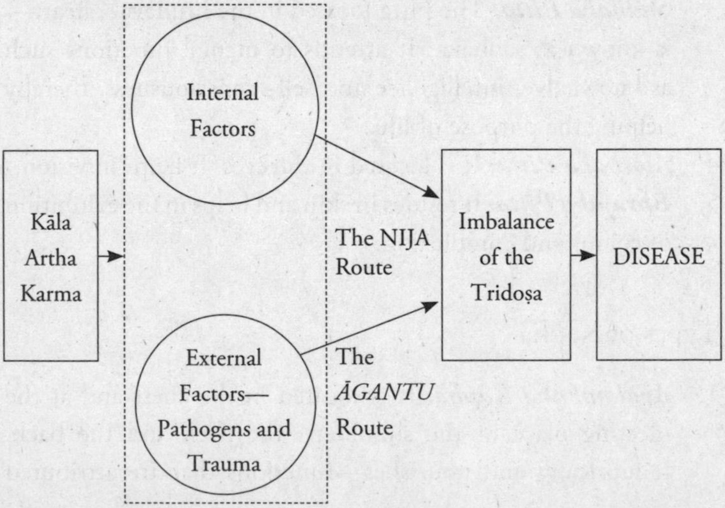

Moderate and appropriate usage of kāla, artha and karma is necessary for good health. Performing seasonal cleaning rituals, using the five senses in moderation and doing appropriate work is important. Imbalanced usage of kāla, artha and karma leads to disease.

The Kāla Factor

Kāla, which means both time and season, can be improper in three ways. It can be less *(hīna)*, more *(athi)* or inappropriate *(mithya)*, leading to doṣa imbalance.

The rainy season is a kāla. For any given geography, this kāla is expected to have a particular duration, in which a certain amount of rainfall is expected. If a place receives less rain, it is the hīna yoga of rain; drought or drought-like conditions can then lead to diseases. If a place receives more rain than expected, it is the athi yoga of rain; flood or flood-like conditions can lead to diseases. If a place receives rain at an inappropriate time or season, it is the mithya yoga, which can also lead to disease.

Thus, the imbalanced usage of kāla causes doṣa imbalance in the human body, leading to diseases.

The Artha Factor

Artha alludes to sensory objects of the material world. Improper usage of sense organs can also lead to the imbalance of doṣa.

An IT professional who sits in front of a computer from 9 a.m.–11 p.m. is doing athi yoga of his eyes. His eyes are tired and strained because of the long hours. He is also doing hīna yoga of his body by sitting in one place for long without any movement. Meanwhile, his improperly used back is experiencing mithya yoga. In totality, sustained behaviour of this kind can easily cause doṣa imbalance, leading to many diseases.

To drive home the lesson, let us take some examples of how artha can be inappropriately used—underused or overused.

Hīna yoga of artha: Here, there is insufficient, scarce or complete lack of connection with objects perceived by our senses. For example, not hearing sounds at all or living in a low-lit area for a long time, consuming very less food, reading books in dim light, etc.

Athi yoga of artha: This is immoderate or excess use of sense organs. For example, staring for long at objects that are minute, bright or intricate; listening to loud music; or excessive eating.

Mithya yoga of artha: This is improper indulgence of our sense organs. For example, seeing or hearing objects that are very frightening, very close, very far or very disgusting—in short, overindulgence of abnormal objects. Other examples would be eating junk food, walking in intense sunlight, etc.

The Karma Factor

Karma means actions or deeds. This includes the way one consumes, sleeps, behaves and thinks. Improper actions also lead to doṣa imbalance.

It is established that activities such as smoking or consuming alcohol are injurious to health. If a person indulges in these excessively, that is improper action or improper karma, which leads to diseases.

Excessive thinking is also bad for health. It dries the body and creates problems. However, many of us take pride in our 'thinking stamina' and cause an imbalance in our system.

To drive home the lesson, let us take some examples of how karma can be inappropriately used: underused or overused.

Hīna yoga of karma: Underuse of speech, physical activity, thinking, etc.

Athi yoga of karma: Excessive speech, physical activity, thinking, etc.

Mithya yoga of karma: Erroneous speech, inappropriate physical activity, improper postures, abrupt jumping and falling, negative thoughts, suppression of natural urges, masking of emotions, etc.

To recapitulate: Hīna, athi or mithya usage of kāla, artha or karma leads to an imbalance in tridoṣa, causing the displacement or accumulation of doṣa. Ayurveda has also mapped out the paths through which the movement (displacement) of doṣa takes place in each ailment. During diagnosis, the pathway through which the doṣa(s) get displaced is understood. And while restoring balance, the doṣa(s) is/are moved back through the same pathway, correcting the problems it/they created, returning it/them to its/their original place, resuming its/their functions and restoring health.

Here's something to ponder: It is said that the wisest acharyas that ever lived were capable of bypassing the doṣas completely—instead, they would address the imbalance at the pañca mahabhūta (elemental) level. But for the rest of the Ayurveda practitioners, the imbalance is addressed at the doṣa level.

Now, having understood the foundational concepts of the tridoṣa and the impact of kāla, artha and karma, we are now ready to understand pathogenesis.

Pathogenesis—the Six Stages of a Disease

In Ayurveda, our acharyas have paid a lot of attention to the manner in which a disease progresses (pathogenesis). Even short-term ailments exhibit stages.

Take fever, for example. Before a rise in temperature, our body might exhibit visible symptoms such as body ache, indigestion, constipation and so on. At this stage, if one takes medicine to bring down the aama in the body, the fever will not manifest at all.

Imagine, therefore, the benefits of identifying a disease in the first or the second stage itself. Ayurveda hopes to make this possible by identifying early-stage biomarkers for each disease. When that happens, an Ayurveda physician can act as the definitive alarm bell, encouraging patients to adopt healthier lifestyles. Of course, the Ayurveda physician already plays this role, but not all practitioners of this fine science are able enough to detect subtle bodily signs that show up in the first or second stage of the disease.

As regards long-term ailments, there are six distinctly identified stages. Let's understand each stage by defining it and taking the example of osteoarthritis:

1. ***Saṁcaya* (accumulation)**: In saṁcaya, the doṣa, which has a place and a role, moves from its place and stops playing its role. Instead, it starts to accumulate.

In sandhi vāta or osteoarthritis, the first stage is identified by the accumulation of vāta in its seat. The causes are vāta—aggravating diet, poor nutrition and improper lifestyle. Trauma or injury in joints and ageing are also possible causes of osteoarthritis. Vāta accumulation happens in the large intestine. Symptoms include indigestion, the fullness of abdomen and feeling cold.

2. ***Prakopa*** **(aggravation)**: At this stage, the accumulated doṣa starts to gets aggravated.

   Improper food consumption and other lifestyle choices lead to the aggravation of vāta and the impairment of pitta and kapha. Even though the vāta is still in the large intestine, an able physician would be able to detect the imbalance at this stage. No additional symptoms are evident at this stage.

3. ***Prasara*** **(spread)**: The accumulated doṣa starts to spread, looking for a weak spot in the body to target.

   In the prasara stage of osteoarthritis, the aggravated vāta, upon reaching saturation at its main site (the large intestine), starts spreading to other parts of the body through different channels and systems. It invades other sites common to vāta (especially bones and joints). As it does so, it causes dryness, lightness, porosity and coarseness in the joints. Since the main function of vāta is to manage motion, including the mobility of the musculoskeletal system, various bones and joints become vulnerable to the gradual accumulation of excess and morbid vāta.

   At this stage, one can do the differential diagnosis of the disease and a proper line of treatment can cure it.

4. ***Sthanasamshraya* (localization)**: The aggravated doṣa now identifies a weak spot in which to settle; localized symptoms appear.

   The morbid, disturbed vāta spreads to different joints and lodges itself in weaker tissues or at the site of obstruction/abnormality in the system. Since the damaged tissues are malnourished, their regeneration does not take place. Pain is felt in the knees and other weight-bearing joints of the body. Joints with maximum musculoskeletal movement are prone to early degeneration. Due to the increased dryness and coarseness of vāta, the kapha in the joints get diminished, further destroying the structure and function of these joints. In addition to pain, the patient may experience swelling, stiffness and difficulty in using the knee joints as designed.

5. ***Vyaktha* (expression)**: Here the disease is fully grown and expresses itself with all its symptoms.

   At this stage, the disease has completely manifested with its cardinal features. Marked symptoms such as intense pain, swelling and crepitus (grating of bone against cartilage) and difficulty in the movements of affected joints become evident. Extension and flexion at the joints become painful. The swelling of the joints resembles a bag filled with air. There is distinctly diminished synovial fluid, degeneration of the cartilage and visible reduced joint space in X-rays.

6. ***Bhedham* (disruption)**: Here, complications increase; with time, treatment of the disease and restoration of the body becomes next to impossible.

The complications of the disease now lead to irreversible changes. Complications may include permanent structural and functional degeneration of the affected joint, with X-rays showing osteophytes, spur and spikes in the bones and loss of cartilage. Pain and stiffness worsen, and treatment procedures barely provide any relief. The individual may also start limping or get dependent on others for their routine work.

Generally, the first three stages go unnoticed as the symptoms are neither stark nor alarming. So patients usually approach a doctor for help in the fourth or the fifth stage of the disease, at which point a complete cure is still possible. The imbalanced doṣa can be sent back to its place and the systems it has affected can be brought back to normalcy. The body can then be restored to a healthy state.

In some diseases, all six stages may take place really fast, but in most diseases, the time taken for the disease to progress from one stage to another is considerable. Lifestyle diseases take time to manifest, not moving from one stage to another for years.

A person may experience full-blown diabetes or cancer today. However, the accumulation would have started ten years ago.

Modern laboratory tests make use of biomarkers (such as a molecule, gene or characteristic) to determine the presence or absence of disease. In many cases, these biomarkers can detect the disease only at stage four or beyond. Much doṣa would have passed under the metaphorical bridge by then. So the restoration process could become long and arduous.

Conclusion

Diseases take time to progress. This puts Ayurveda in a winning position, given its ability to detect early warning signs in the body.

If Ayurveda and modern science come together and find early-stage biomarkers of diseases, drastic changes in healthcare management and disease prevention are possible.

4

Prakṛti and the Genome

Even those casually acquainted with Ayurveda know the overarching role played by prakṛti in this healthcare system. The treatment of a patient begins with identifying their prakṛti. From that point, all medicines that are given to the patient take into account their prakṛti.

For centuries, Ayurveda successfully used prakṛti to customize healthcare and manage lifestyle. But once the Western world developed the allopathic model, their scientists asked our acharyas some confounding questions:

How do you prove the existence of prakṛti?

Can you put it under a microscope?

Can you mix it with something else in a test tube?

Well, that wasn't possible. Therefore, many sceptics and cynics in the Western world dismissed Ayurveda as pseudoscience.

All that changed in 2015, when one of the most prestigious scientific journals in the world, *Nature*, published a paper titled

'Genome-Wide Analysis Correlates Ayurveda Prakṛti'. The paper was authored by twenty-three professionals from the life sciences and, biomedical and Ayurveda scientists,* including yours truly. It successfully mapped prakṛti to genes. In other words, it mapped the concept, the existence of which was disputed. And since *Nature* published the paper, the world sat up and took notice.

Before we delve into the details of the study, let's explore the concept of prakṛti some more—for the benefit of the newly curious and the timelessly curious.

Characteristics of Prakṛti

We have already understood the role of prakṛti in maintaining balance in the body. Now let's look at the personality of prakṛti:

Assessment Is Required to Determine Prakṛti

An Ayurvedic physician studies or observes about seventy factors—of the physical, physiological, psychological and behavioural realms— to ascertain one's prakṛti. Some questions or traits are given higher weightage as they are very important indicators of prakṛti. In fact, some factors are so important that they, by themselves, can determine the prakṛti of the person.

* Periyasamy Govindaraj, Sheikh Nizamuddin, Anugula Sharath, Vuskamalla Jyothi, Harish Rotti, Ritu Raval, Jayakrishna Nayak, Balakrishna K. Bhat, B.V. Prasanna, Pooja Shintre, Mayura Sule, Kalpana S. Joshi, Amrish P. Dedge, Ramachandra Bharadwaj, G.G. Gangadharan, Sreekumaran Nair, Puthiya M. Gopinath, Bhushan Patwardhan, Paturu Kondaiah, Kapaettu Satyamoorthy, Marthanda Varma Sankaran Valiathan and Kumarasamy Thangaraja.

Prakṛti Doesn't Change

Like a person's blood group, it will remain the same throughout their lives.

In the very first chapter of the *Ashtanga Hrudayam Sutra Sthana*, the ninth and tenth slokas deal with the eternal nature of an individual's prakṛti.

Shukraarthavasthaih janmamaadou visheneeva vishakrimeh |
Taihi cha tisrah prakrutayo hīnamadhyaottamaah pruthak |
Samadhathuh samastaasu shrestaa nindyaa dwidoṣajaah

—*Ashtanga Hrudayam Sutra Sthana, Chapter 1, Slokas 9 and 10*

This sloka states that the doṣas, which are present in the *sukra* (sperm) and *ārtava* (ovum) at the time of fertilization, combine and undergo a change in their proportions. If the three doṣas are in equal proportion, it is called *samadhātu* prakṛti—this is the ideal scenario and will be called *uttama* (strong). If there are two predominant doṣas or only one predominant doṣa in the prakṛti, it can be madhyama (moderate strength) or hīna (weak). Interestingly, the phenomenon of the creation of prakṛti is likened to the survival of poisonous worms, which, as born from poison, don't die from it. Similarly, prakṛti formed from doṣa continues to manifest in the person for as long as they live.

Prakṛti Cannot Be Identified at Birth

Even though the prakṛti of a person gets decided at the time of conception, it cannot be identified before the age of sixteen. This is because some of the physical characteristics and secondary sexual characteristics become evident only after attaining puberty.

Gut flora evolves in the first few years, and therefore the prakṛti of the *koshta* (gut) is still being defined. And since these factors play a role in deciding the prakṛti, it is imperative to wait until the age of sixteen or thereabouts.

One or More Doṣas Can Dominate Prakṛti

Humankind can be divided into seven types of prakṛti:

- Only a single prominent doṣa:
  1. *Vāta prakṛti*
  2. *Pitta prakṛti*
  3. *Kapha prakṛti*

- Two prominent doṣas:
  4. *Vāta–pitta prakṛti*
  5. *Pitta–kapha prakṛti*
  6. *Kapha–vāta prakṛti*

- Comparable influence of all three doṣas:
  7. *Vāta–pitta–kapha prakṛti*

If a person has more than 60 per cent of one doṣa, it is called the prominent prakṛti of that person. When no doṣa has more than 60 per cent, the person's prakṛti is made up of two prominent doṣas or, in rare instances, a combination of all three doṣas. As already mentioned, an equal combination of all three doṣas is said to be the best prakṛti.

Prakṛti and the DNA Connection

The idea that prakṛti can be associated with DNA and, in turn, our genes, is exciting as it establishes a connection between an age-old scientific practice and the modern proof-oriented scientific process. With this in mind, the team of Ayurveda physicians (mentioned in the footnote on p.52) made a plan, developed a hypothesis and started their research.

The salient features of the research project were as follows:

A Wide Diversity of Subjects

At Ayurveda research centres in Bangalore, Pune and Udupi, 3416 healthy male subjects between the ages of twenty and thirty were screened. The participants belonged to different ethnic and linguistic groups and hailed from different geographies. They did not smoke or have chronic afflictions such as diabetes and hypertension. They were healthy and their blood pressure was normal. They also did not have a history of infectious diseases in the recent past. Several other tests were conducted, and checks and measures were taken to ensure that the blood-sample selection was random and free of biases.

Women Were Excluded as Subjects

Women were excluded from the study for specific reasons. Blood drawn from the participants would be used for multiple research projects. Menstruating women experience hormonal changes throughout the month—especially before and after ovulation, and before and after menstruation—and these fluctuations might have compromised the study.

It needs to be noted that, although this particular study avoided the participation of women subjects, many other research projects do include them.

Prakṛti Identification Involved a Three-Layer Check

- First, a senior Ayurveda physician asked each of the 3416 male subjects all the assessment questions to identify the prakṛti.
- Secondly, a software application developed by CDAC—Ayusoft—was used directly by the subjects to enter all the information. The software then determined the prakṛti of the subject.
- Finally, an Ayurveda physician, unaware of the first two processes, did a comparison of the results. Only the subjects whose results from the software matched the results from the physician were considered for the study.

Using this process, 262 of the 3416 samples were selected for the study. All of them had only a single prominent doṣa and were otherwise randomly selected. In the final reckoning, the research sample had ninety-four subjects with a prominent vāta prakṛti, seventy-five with a prominent pitta prakṛti and ninety-three with a prominent kapha prakṛti.

Research Results

Fifty-two gene markers were identified to be descriptive of prakṛti. These genes carry information that determines the prakṛti of a person. One's prakṛti can now be identified by studying their genes. The presence or absence of some of the genes out of these fifty-two will determine the prakṛti of the person. It was thus established that prakṛti is connected to genes and can be identified through gene markers.

The Impact

The magnitude of the breakthrough achieved by this research project cannot be underestimated. Overall, the following benefits have been accrued:

- The research proved that Ayurveda concepts have a scientific basis. While not exactly cutting-edge, modern research has taken place in Ayurveda; such endeavours can be made possible, given time, effort and the presence of talented Ayurveda champions.
- It instilled confidence in Ayurveda practitioners as the research paper was not challenged after being published in *Nature*
- A bridge was built between ancient science and the world of modern research.

Conclusion

Since time immemorial, Ayurveda has used prakṛti to customize healthcare by:

- Changing medicine given to people of different prakṛti.
- Suggesting prakṛti-appropriate nutrition and lifestyle (we shall explore this in detail later).

In other words, prakṛti has been a pivotal consideration in the prevention of disease and promotion of health.

There is no reason why allopathy cannot leverage this breakthrough in its own healthcare system. After all, doctors use biomarkers to identify medications and procedures that are unsuitable for a given patient. Perhaps some time in the near future, they will be able to use the fifty-two gene markers identified as unique to prakṛti while diagnosing a patient and prescribing a treatment.

As for the Ayurveda community, this project has provided it with the confidence to deliver whenever evidence is demanded by sceptics. They now know that evidence can be produced. Their abstract concepts can be distilled into tangible and observable results.

It's the best time for Ayurveda and modern science to come together. We will explore this further in the chapter 'The Summative Approach'.

Tailor-made healthcare, as it stands today, is in its very nascent stage of development. The concept of prakṛti shows the way forward.

5

Gut, GIT and Microbiome

It's 2011. In the Mayo Clinic in Scottsdale, Arizona, a surgeon prepares to implement a procedure he has never before attempted. His patient is a thirty-three-year-old man who has been bleeding from his rectum for the past six months. His gut has been taken over by *Clostridium difficile*, a pathogen notorious for more or less wiping out the good bacteria in the gastrointestinal tract. Today's procedure is a Hail Mary for the patient—either it will succeed or he will die.

When the time is nigh, the surgeon infuses the patient's wife's faecal matter—mixed in saline solution and filtered to remove solids—into the patient's colon!

Disgusting as the procedure sounds, it works like magic. A man who could barely sit down walks out of the clinic in a matter of days—reborn by the miracle that is his wife's faeces.

The acceptance of fecal microbiota transplantation (FMT) by the renowned Mayo Clinic kick-started the USA's acceptance of the procedure. Since then, the Mayo Clinic alone has conducted hundreds of FMTs and enjoyed an approximate success rate of

90 per cent. This, despite the Food and Drug Administration's (FDA's) reluctance to embrace FMT. In fact, the FDA initially deemed FMT procedures equivalent to trial drugs. Hence, approval required a mountain of paperwork, and this dissuaded most doctors and surgeons from attempting FMT. Thankfully, unimpeachable statistics forced the FDA to accept FMT as a procedure that needs to be used with discretion. Like a reluctant child biting into boiled broccoli, the FDA overcame its disgust to achieve long-term gains.

When I read the about the Mayo Clinic embracing what was, until then, a ridiculed procedure, I smiled. Many years ago, I had seen a tribal doctor in the jungles of Wayanad perform a similar 'miracle'. A man had come to him with intense diarrhoea and severe dehydration. Without blinking an eyelid, the doctor gave him a small jaggery-coloured pellet. The diarrhoea stopped in a couple of hours.

'What was the substance in the pellet?' I had asked him.

Reluctantly, after much prodding, he had revealed that it was the dried faeces of a healthy dog encapsulated in solid jaggery!

Ancient Indian and Chinese healthcare practitioners have known that a gastrointestinal tract, or GIT, colonized by a diverse population of helpful microorganisms can stave off most pathogens that invade us through our GIT. If the gut is the body's second brain, these trillions of microorganisms—together known as microbiota or microbiome—are its neurons.

Centuries after learning to use yeast as a cooking aid, we are learning more about the supportive role played by the human microbiome, which constitutes our gut flora. A great number of lifestyle diseases—such as colorectal cancer, colon cancer, irritable bowel syndrome, obesity and diabetes—can be kept at bay simply by taking care of our gut and gut flora.

It's time we said hello to the least visible and most underrated soldiers of health.

GIT—the Highway of Life

The gastrointestinal tract begins at the mouth and ends at the anus. The GIT is perhaps the most intricately designed highway we've seen.

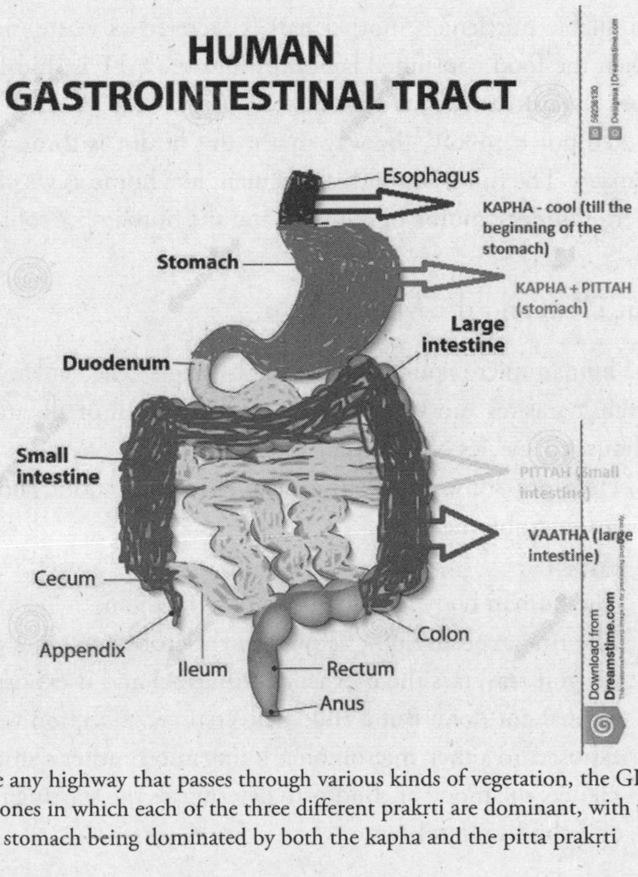

Like any highway that passes through various kinds of vegetation, the GIT has zones in which each of the three different prakṛti are dominant, with the stomach being dominated by both the kapha and the pitta prakṛti

At the beginning of the highway, we see intelligent collaboration between the teeth and the mouth—they use sharp edges and saliva, respectively, to break down food. After that comes the epiglottis, which acts as a no-entry signboard, keeping food out of the windpipe. Upon crossing that point, food passes through an acidic furnace (stomach) and two processing plants (the small and large intestines).

As the food journeys through the GIT highway, it is broken down. A part of it is converted into usable energy and assimilable nutrients. Another part is excreted as waste matter. When the food consumed is healthy and the GIT is shipshape, most diseases are kept at bay.

To put it mildly, the way to a man's health is through his stomach. The full truth of this statement hits home as we obtain a better understanding of gut flora and the human microbiome.

Gut Flora and the Microbiome

The human microbiome includes yeasts, single-celled eukaryotes, certain parasites and viruses and, most important of all, around a thousand species of bacteria.

Here are some interesting facts about gut flora and the human microbiome:

- The human body is home to trillions of them.
- The first exposure of a baby to the microbiome takes place when it traverses the mother's birth canal and is exposed to vaginal gut flora. But a child delivered via C-section will be exposed to other microbiome lining the mother's midriff. Hence, the mode of childbirth determines the starting point of a child's microbiome.

- By the age of two, a child's microbiome starts resembling the one they will have as an adult. Sources of these microorganisms include the air, breast milk, food, etc. At any point in a person's life, they can affect some amount of change in their GIT flora by changing their diet and lifestyle.
- Barring pathogens, all GIT flora is extremely useful to human beings, as they:
  - Help break down dietary fibre.
  - Synthesize certain vitamins such as B and K.
  - Prevent the growth of harmful species of microbiome.
  - Help convert waste into stool.

  In short, they keep the GIT running like a well-oiled machine, so long as they outnumber pathogens by a minimum ratio of 4:1.
- Ninety per cent of all gut bacteria comes from only thirty to forty species. Yet, there is great variation in gut flora between individuals of different races, dietary habits and lifestyles.

  A study found African children to have a more diverse set of gut flora as compared to European children. This increases their ability to digest tough food and, as a corollary, consume fewer calories to gain the same amount of energy. Intolerance to certain food groups is due to the absence of certain kinds of microorganisms (we'll explore this in detail later in this chapter).
- The greatest density of microorganisms is found in the large intestine, where some estimates suggest the presence of 10^{12} cells per gram of intestinal content.

The estimated ratio of microbiome cells to human cells in the human body has been fluctuating in the past decade.

On the higher end, this ratio is estimated to be 10. On the lower end, it is 1.1. So to the best of our knowledge, the ratio must be 10:1.1.

There seems to be no doubt that microbial cells outnumber human cells. Think about that for a moment. The majority of a human being is non-human! And since our microbiome is determined by our diet and lifestyle, the axiom 'You are what you eat' assumes a deeper meaning.

The Abuse of Microbiome

Given that our microbes outnumber the rest of us, is it any surprise that they play a huge role in keeping us healthy? One study describes this role succinctly by stating, 'Interactions between the microbiota and the host immune system are numerous, complex and bidirectional.' Simply put, there seems to be a synergistic exchange of information between microbes and our immune system.

We are just about beginning to understand the complexity and depth of this synergy. But we already know that gut microbes can influence a person's food habits, moods, desires, cravings and, therefore, health. In other words, our microbiome influences our physical, physiological and emotional well-being. So it is important to keep our microbes happy, for they will have the same effect on us.

While science tells us that we need to respect our microbiome, in reality, we knowingly or unknowingly abuse our microscopic friends. Here are a few ways in which we impact the diversity and numbers of our gut flora:

1. **Dietary habits**

- Consumption of junk food, processed food and lack of fibre in food depletes flora.
- Our flora can vary, depending on the staple grain we consume—be it rice, wheat, quinoa, barley, ragi or some other millet.
- Even the staple grain we consume is processed to an extent. For instance, when white rice gets polished, it loses the fibrous outer covering that provides nutrients and roughage. Prolonged consumption of such non-fibrous, starchy rice will deplete gut flora.

2. **Lifestyle**

   By this, we allude to stress, the hours we keep, the hours we sleep, our daily physical activities, etc.

3. **Disease**

   Certain diseases impact our dietary habits, lifestyle and bowel function. They, thereby, impact our gut flora.

4. **Medication (Antibiotics)**

   Broad-spectrum antibiotics can result in the depletion of gut flora and a spurt in the number of pathogenic bacteria. This will affect the body's ability to digest food.

   So carpet-bombing the gut with antibiotics can sometimes be akin to burning down the crops to protect them from locusts.

That analogy is quite apt. The moment we start treating our gut flora—our microbiome—as part of our wealth, our entire approach to GIT healthcare will change.

Lactose and Gluten Intolerance

Intolerance to a food group can be inherited through genes or might be developed over a period of time due to diet or other lifestyle issues. It stands to reason that the intolerance is due to the absence of certain flora that help digest that particular food—be it gluten, lactose or something else. Here are proactive measures you can take to become tolerant to that food:

- Create a mashi (ash) of a small amount of the substance, dissolve it in water and drink it.
- Consume foods that will rebuild the missing gut flora.
- Consume small quantities of the food (wheat or milk) to regenerate the missing gut flora.
- Consult a physician to determine whether pañca karma (the fivefold detoxification therapy), such as *snehapana* (medicated ghee) and/or *virechana* (medicine-induced purgation), will work for you.
- Consume probiotic supplements—there is no harm in trying this unlikely cure.
- Lactose-intolerant people could also try A2 type of milk, which is produced by non-hybrid indigenous breeds of cattle.
- For really desperate situations, we have the highly reliable FMT.

In short, there is no need to treat intolerance to particular food groups as a life-imprisonment sentence. We just need to find a way to re-colonize our gut with the appropriate flora.

Ayurveda and Gut Flora

Ayurveda has long understood the importance of gut and gut microbes. We know this because:

1. Of the ten factors that Ayurveda considers while offering customized healthcare to an individual, six have a direct bearing on gut flora. These include:

- *Deśam*—the body of the patient, plus the geography of the place, which determines dietary patterns of the populace.
- *Kāla*—season/time. Medicines have to be digested just like food, and seasons influence our digestive abilities.
- *Anala*—the digestive fire, which varies from one individual to another, and is influenced by gut flora.
- *Vaya*—the age of the patient, which determines the diversity and maturity of the individual's gut flora.
- *Sātmya*—the general habits (lifestyle) of the person.
- *Āhāra*—dietary habits, which has a direct bearing on the diversity and health of our gut flora.

2. *Koshta* (the gut) is the only part of the body that has its own prakṛti! This tells us that the gut was seen to have its own unique personality. Many treatments have been devised to address imbalances in the koshta.
3. All Ayurvedic medicines are friendly towards gut flora. Medicines such as *triphala* not only fight indigestion but help the gut flora flourish.
4. Basti (enema) is a key treatment methodology to address koshta imbalances. Some acharyas say that the impact

of basti treatments is the same as the impact of all other Ayurveda treatments put together. Seen in that context, at least half of the science of Ayurveda has been designed to keep the gut functioning well. Hence, we give special emphasis to basti treatments later in the chapter.

Triphala, the Eleven-Way Wonder

Triphala is a magic medicine that can be used in eleven ways:

1. With sugar—treats acid peptic disorders.
2. With hot water—as laxative.
3. With honey—for kapha doṣa diseases.
4. With ghee—for pitta doṣa diseases.
5. With rock salt—for vāta doṣa diseases.
6. As plain powder—for gum diseases.
7. As black ash—for asthma.
8. As kaṣāya—for liver damages.
9. As oil—for non-healing ulcers.
10. As face pack—to address complexion problems.
11. With unequal parts of ghee and honey—for promoting eyesight.

Concept to Practice

Now that we have seen the importance Ayurveda places upon gut flora and the human microbiome, let's list out simple ways in which we can convert knowledge into practice on a daily basis:

- Ensure you consume a good amount of fibre in every meal. If you must eat a starchy grain such as rice, switch to red rice, which retains the fibre from the enveloping husk.
- Have a diet full of variety:
  - o Meals must consist of every food group (grains, vegetables, fruits, pulses and, for non-vegetarians, a small portion of meat).
  - o Instead of sticking to just one staple foodgrain, you can try many, such as rice, wheat, quinoa, barley, ragi and other millets. However, bear in mind that the body will take some time to adjust to food it has never before consumed. Some people may even experience constipation, frequent hunger, etc.
- Avoid soft drinks and other junk food that have the power to erode the gut flora due to prolonged usage.
- Avoid food that is inadvisable for your specific prakṛti.
- Consume food of all the six tastes, dominated by sweet (more details of the six tastes are available in the 'Tailor-Made Healthcare' chapter).
- Sip lukewarm water frequently between meals.
- Consume only fresh and warm food.
  - o Reheated food is like slow poison.
  - o Start meals with a spoonful of ghee and end them with fresh thick buttermilk—prepared by churning diluted curds and removing the butter. Such buttermilk will be light, astringent and can pacify kapha and vāta. It goes a long way in addressing ailments such as oedema, piles, pancreatic disorders, colicky pain, irritable bowel syndrome, diarrhoea, urinary problems, loss of taste, bloated abdomen, splenic disorders and anaemia.

- Do not consume curds daily and never at night.
- Fill half the stomach with solids, a quarter with fluids and leave the rest vacant for gaseous exchanges.
- Don't eat anything between meals.
- Consume probiotic supplements. While they have proven health benefits, probiotic supplements do not alter faecal microbiota composition in any way. So we cannot see it as a panacea.

The practice of keeping the gut clean is perhaps best illustrated by this sloka:

Sheetodbhavam doṣachayamvasanthe
Vishodhayan greeshmajam abhrakaale |
Ghanaathyayee vaarshikamaashusamyak
Praapnoti rogaanrutujaanna jaatu||

—*Ashtanga Hrudayam Sutra Sthana, Chapter 4, Sloka 34*

This sloka says that we must cleanse our gut at the beginning of each season. The accumulation of the doṣa during the cold season should be expelled during spring and that arising from summer should be expelled during the rainy season. Similarly, doṣa arising in the rainy season should be expelled in autumn expeditiously and effectively. Thus, people will not become victims of diseases borne by the effect of the seasons.

A Case Study

Let's look at a case study that illustrates the holism of the Ayurvedic approach.

A forty-five-year-old man approached us with irritable bowel syndrome. His symptoms were mucous stools, abdominal cramps, bloated abdomen, tiredness and a burning sensation in the abdomen.

We identified him as having the pitta prakṛti, which meant that his body had an excess of the fire element. The stomach, therefore, tended to be more acidic than was good for him. Our examination also revealed that he had *mrudukoshta*, which meant that his stools were soft and he tended to pass them more often.

He had been suffering for over five years and allopathic medicines had not helped. Our course of treatment was as follows:

- He was given medicines for igniting his digestive fire and digestion.
- Medicated ghee was prescribed to soothe the stomach and heal the inner lining of his intestine.
- A full-body massage was given to make him relax, enhance his blood circulation—and hence his metabolism.
- Later, rasāyana medicines were given to rejuvenate his digestive system.
- Diet and lifestyle changes were suggested. He was asked to avoid maida and spicy food. He was also asked to keep regular hours.

It's been a year since his treatment began. He has been keeping well and is managing his ailment with only oral medication.

In the case study given above, basti was not used at all. However, it is the biggest tool at our disposal for GIT problems. Mahatma Gandhi himself advocated bastis as pathways to good health. Ayurveda tells us why he was such a big fan of the concept.

Basti—the Champion Purifier

If you put basti on one pan of a measuring scale and all other Ayurveda treatments on the other, the scale will balance out. Such is the potency and significance of basti.

Basti, or medicated enema, is a pañca karma treatment. Pañca karma is a detoxification process that uses five techniques—*vamana* (emesis), virechana (purgation), *nasya* (nasal inhalation of medicine), basti (medicated enema) and *raktamokṣaṇa* (bloodletting).

Charaka says that basti cleanses and/or treats the guts, and in turn, the whole body. He explained basti in the simplest way possible:

> Imagine a shepherd living in a village close to the forest. Every morning, he packs his lunch and walks into the forest with his herd. The cows spread to different parts of the forest, especially the green ends, and graze. The whole day, the cows graze and roam to their heart's content. In the evening, when it is time to return, the shepherd takes out his flute and plays it. Cows, which have wandered far, hear the sound of the flute and come back to him. Together, they return home.
>
> —*Charaka Samhita, Siddhi Sthana*

If we take our body to be the forest, the cows are all the vitiated doṣas. And the sound of the flute is the *veeryam* (effect/power) of the basti's decoction, which spreads all over the body and brings all the vitiated doṣas into the rectum, so that it can get expelled.

That is the power of basti. It has the capacity to reach all parts of the body and expel everything that causes doṣa imbalances via the rectum.

Types of Basti

Let's have a look at what the classification of basti is based upon:

1. Site of administration
2. Type of medicine used
3. Function
4. Number of bastis

These classifications are sub-divided as follows:

1. **Site of administration**
   a. *Pakwashaya gata:* The medicine is administered into the gut (large intestine) through the anal route. This basti helps bring down and balance the vāta doṣa. This is the best treatment for all vāta-predominant and single-vāta diseases.
   b. *Garbhashaya gata:* In this, the medicine is administered through the vaginal route to treat reproductive disorders.
   c. *Mutrashaya gata:* The medicine is administered through the urethral route, for both men and women. This is to treat urogenital disorders. The enema given through the urinary or genital passage is called *uttara* basti.
   d. *Vrana gata:* Medicinal liquids are pushed into the wounds, ulcers and sinuses. This is called *vrana* basti. It helps clean and heal the wounds and ulcers.

Note: *Janu* basti, *kati* basti, etc., are external oil treatments and have nothing to do with classical basti.

2. **Type of medicine used**

a. *Niruha basti,* kaṣāya *basti* or *asthapana basti:* Here, kaṣāya or herbal decoction is used. Since this basti expels morbid doṣa and/or diseases from the body, it is called niruha basti (niruha = to eliminate; also means that its effects are unpredictable or unmeasurable). And since it enhances life span (*ayus*), it is called asthapana basti. The dosage of niruha basti varies according to age and the maximum dosage is said to be 1152 grams.

b. *Madhu-tailika basti:* It is a variant of niruha basti. As the name indicates, apart from other medicaments, *madhu* (honey) and *taila* (oil) are used as the main ingredients of the basti medicine. It is also known as *yapana* basti, *siddha* basti and *yuktaratha* basti.

c. *Anuvasana basti:* The word '*anuvasana*' means 'to stay'. In anuvasana basti, the administered medicines—medicated fats, mainly oils and/or ghee (*sneha*)—stays for a longer duration inside the intestine (bladder, uterus). This basti can be administered on a daily basis.

Depending on the quantity (dosage) of sneha administered, anuvasana basti is divided into three types. They are:

i. *Agrya mātrā basti*—the dosage of sneha basti will be ¼ the dosage of niruha for a given age (288 grams).

ii. The *madhyama mātrā* (moderate or intermediate dosage) of sneha basti is 144 grams.

iii. The *kaniyasi mātrā* (lowest dosage) of sneha basti is 72 grams.

3. **Function**
   a. *Shodhana basti:* The word '*shodhana*' means 'to cleanse'. So this basti mainly acts to expel morbid doṣa and excreta from the body.
   b. *Lekhana basti:* '*Lekhana*' means 'scraping'. Lekhana basti scrapes off excessive fat that has accumulated in the body. This helps the patient slim down and is thus used effectively in treating obesity and related metabolic and hormonal disorders.
   c. *Snehana basti:* The word '*snehana*' means 'to cause unctuousness or to provide oiliness or lubrication'. This basti helps in lubrication of each and every cell of the body.
   d. *Brimhana basti:* The word '*brimhana*' means 'to promote bulk of the body', mainly to enhance the quality and bulk of muscles. This term can be generalized to mean the enhancement of all tissues, not just muscles.

4. **Number of bastis**
   a. *Karma basti:* In this, a total of thirty bastis are given—eighteen anuvasana bastis and twelve niruha bastis.
   b. *Kāla basti:* In this, a total of sixteen bastis are given. Six niruha bastis and ten anuvasana bastis are administered over a period of sixteen days.
   c. *Yoga basti:* In this, a total of eight bastis are given. In yoga basti, three niruha bastis and five anuvasana bastis are administered over a period of eight days.

Other types of bastis include:

1. *Utkleshana basti:* The word '*utkleshana*' means 'to provoke'. This basti provokes morbid doṣa and *malas* (excreta) in the body, and enhances their quantity by liquefying them. As a result, it becomes easier to flush them out of the body.
2. *Doṣahara basti:* The word '*doṣahara*' means 'to eliminate morbid doṣa'. It serves the purpose of shodhana type of niruha basti.
3. *Shaman basti:* The word '*shamana*' means 'to pacify'. Shaman basti helps suppress or pacify the vitiated doṣa and bring it/them back to normalcy.

Other types of basti (based on functions) explained by Charaka:

1. *Vātaghna basti:* Destroys the morbid/vitiated vāta.
2. *Bala-varnakrit basti:* Enhances *bala* (strength and immunity) and *varna* (colour and texture).
3. *Snehaneeya basti:* Provides lubrication and unctuousness to cells.
4. *Shukrakrit basti:* Enhances the quality and quantity of semen.
5. *Krimighna basti:* Helps destroy and expel troublemaking microorganisms (*krimi*).
6. *Vrishatvakrit basti:* Enhances sexual potency and libido; cures impotency.

The gamut of basti treatments underlines the fact that Charaka's understanding of the human body was impeccable. They focused on things that mattered the most.

In addition to removing toxins from the body, bastis also help the gut flora flourish. In fact, medicines inserted into the anus reach the gut flora directly. They, thereby, assist in changing the combination of gut flora and help it grow.

Conclusion

It can be said that the GIT, not the brain, is the true master of the human body. The GIT maintains the body's dynamic equilibrium and keeps us at our healthiest best.

In the near future, we might have a deeper understanding of the microbiome–human relationship. This might help us devise novel microbiome-centric therapies for various ailments. Want to quit an addiction? Rebuild the 'X' type of microbes in the gut. Feeling depressed? Enhance those 'Y' microbes! And so on . . .

Meanwhile, we have gut-friendly Ayurveda medicines and gut-friendly basti procedures to set things back in order.

6

Epigenetics*

In his riveting TEDx talk titled 'How to Practise Emotional Hygiene', psychologist Guy Winch takes us on a journey that describes his evolving relationship with his identical twin brother. The two led very different lives after Guy Winch left his home in Europe to pursue his education in the USA. The relationship reached a crisis when the brother was diagnosed with Stage III non-Hodgkin's lymphoma. His cancer developed aggressively. At this juncture, though in physical pain, Winch's brother seemed to handle his emotions a lot better than Winch himself. Winch resorted to rumination and constant exposure to severe emotional pain. Fortunately, this story ends happily, with the brother making a full recovery.

For a scientist, an interesting question emerges out of this story: Why did the twins, who share nearly 100 per cent of their DNA, end up with such different destinies in the area of health?

---

* Please read this chapter in conjunction with the next, titled 'Pillars of Restoration: Prevention and Promotion'.

Indeed, why do a majority of identical twins begin diverging in matters of health, physical appearance, likes and dislikes, intellect, career growth, sexual behaviour and a hundred other parameters? It stands to reason that genes don't write our destinies. Perhaps genes offer a range of destinies and some other force then makes us choose one of the destinies available to us.

Welcome to epigenetics—an exciting field that explores a phenomenon that's over and beyond genetics. In a nutshell, epigenetic studies focus on how and why genes express themselves. Only when a gene is expressed does it affect the destiny of the host body. Even here, a gene can be triggered either by a biological on–off switch or a knob like mechanism that increases or decreases the level of the gene expression.

Unhealthy lifestyles, dysfunctional ecosystems and negative life experiences can help the expression of genes that are harmful to us. For instance, consumption of sugary food might accelerate the expression of 'diabetic genes' in those who are prone to diabetes.

On the other hand, a lifestyle that pays homage to mental and physical well-being can keep many harmful gene expressions at bay, including the dreaded set of diabetic genes.

Come to think of it, epigenetics is the latest interpretation of how the human body works. In prehistoric times, diseases were believed to be the work of evil spirits. When we invented God, we ascribed our diseases to His wrath. At the dawn of scientific thinking, we understood the link between pathogens and diseases. And then came the human genome project, which helped us link so much of our destiny to genes. Fortunately, before we drew a fatalistic outlook to life, along came epigenetics, teaching us that we are as much in control of our destinies as our genes, if not more.

Seen in this context, epigenetics is not only the latest but also the most accurate theory of how the human body works.

While discussing epigenetics, we must keep in mind that the next generation is likely to inherit our expressed genes, leading to intergenerational similarities in physical health and behavioural characteristics. In short, the battle with unhealthy genes can potentially last beyond one's own lifetime. If we have an unhealthy lifestyle, which triggers the expression of harmful genes, our children might also suffer the consequences.

This belief should come with a disclaimer. Follicles that develop into mature eggs in the female are created at birth and will therefore carry birth-time gene expression, but a father's sperm is produced daily and is, therefore, more flexible in passing on better genes developed through healthier life choices.

Before epigenetics, we thought that the best way to get rid of diseases was to snip off the body part responsible for the disease, if it were possible at all. Ovaries and uteruses are removed by women who have family histories of cancer in these body parts. One of the most famous celebrity surgeries in recent times is that of Angelina Jolie, who got her breasts removed. While there is a definite benefit of surgical removal, side-effects in the form of hormonal imbalances can impair quality of life.

With epigenetic knowledge, we can now create better ways of keeping diseases at bay. In an alternate universe, Angelina Jolie visits an expert doctor at the age of, say, sixteen, and is given a fool-proof lifestyle formula so that she never has breast cancer.

That is the power of epigenetics. Let's look at how it has leveraged this concept before it came into vogue.

Ayurveda and Epigenetics

> Balee Purushakaroo Hi Daivamapyativartate ||
>
> —*Ashtanga Hrudayam, Shareera Sthana, 1*

The rough translation of the above sloka, taken from an ancient Ayurveda text, is that actions taken by a human being are stronger than the destiny prescribed by God. If we were to accept reincarnation as truth, this sloka would mean that appropriate actions taken at appropriate times in this lifetime might be more powerful than the effects of previous lives. I was a student when I read this, and I was puzzled. How could this be? However, my practice of Ayurveda continuously brought home the wisdom of this sloka. The advent of epigenetics, of course, proved that this sloka contained an idea way ahead of its time.

At the time of conception, the prakṛti of the human being is determined as soon as the zygote is formed, although some parts of the prakṛti are not expressed until the age of sixteen. Like modern science, Ayurveda refused to be fatalistic about the human being's chances of living a long and happy life. Instead of blaming genes, Ayurveda advocated seeing genes as the raw materials of life. The nature of the raw material determines the kind of lifestyle that one must lead.

We see here a desire to make nurture triumph over nature. And the claiming of a glorious life begins before the birth of the child. It begins with how a mother and the foetus are nurtured during pregnancy.

Epigenetics Begins at the Beginning

In the evening preceding my birth, one of our cows came home late. Around 10 p.m., my mother went to the cattle shed to milk the latecomer. As she was doing so, she felt what later emerged to be the beginning of labour pain. She finished her chores and walked into the room usually used for childbirth. Somebody was sent to fetch the midwife, who arrived just in time to cut the umbilical cord.

Like my mother, a great number of women of that generation underwent natural and easy childbirth. Today, we have turned pregnancy into a disease and childbirth into an experience governed by panic.

By going back to the accumulated wisdom of Ayurveda, we can again make pregnancy a joyous celebration of life. Here is what we can do:

Phase	**Action Item(s)**
Pre-pregnancy	The couple eager to conceive should change their diet and use rejuvenation techniques to help the production of healthy reproductive tissues. **Food**: • They should consume *satvika* foods, which are fresh, light and easy to digest. At the same time, they nourish and balance all the dhātu and the mind. • The woman should consume ghee and black gram preparations, rice, milk and milk preparations, and other foods with a predominantly sweet taste. **Behaviour**: • Both the man and the woman should have observed celibacy for a month. • Both should keep their minds calm and happy at all times with the help of profuse oil therapies.

	• They should be reunited (after the period of celibacy) on the fourth day after the onset of menstruation, after being blessed by the family deity, elders and priest.
First trimester	The objective is to keep the foetus in the womb because many miscarriages happen in the first trimester due to a weak uterus. Specific food and medicines are to be given to the pregnant lady to keep the baby safe and strong. These include cold milk in small quantities, consumed frequently, *madhura** (sweet) foods, *sheeta* (cooling to the body) foods, and a lot of fluids. Herbs such as *yashtimadhu* (Glyverrhizaglabra), *chandana* (white sandalwood) and *raktachandana* (red sandalwood) are also advisable.
Second trimester	Pamper the expectant mother. Keep her healthy and happy. Help her follow a specific regimen of very mild exercises and no massages. Milk and milk products with rice, sugar, butter, fruits (such as pomegranate and *amla*) and bulk-promoting food for the growth of the foetus is advised. Strength-promoting and complexion-promoting medicinal herbs such as bala and ashwagandha are helpful.
Third trimester	Massages to aid a natural birth are given on the last week of the expected day of delivery without any pressure, only to soften the abdominal muscles. Special food is given to help the mother reach full term. These include ghee, rice and asparagus. Less salt is preferred. Herbs such as *gokshura* (*Tribulus terrestris*), prishniparni (*Uraria picta*), bala (*Sida cordifolia*) and vidarikanda (*Peuraria tuberose*) are helpful. Some medicated oil enemas *(*mātrā basti*)* or tampons are suggested to soften the vaginal passage for easy delivery.

* Foods have one of six rasas, or tastes, namely *madhura* (sweet), *amla* (sour), *lavana* (salty), *tikta* (bitter), *ooshna* (spicy) and *kaṣāyaka* (astringent). These are discussed in detail in the chapter 'Tailor-Made Healthcare'.

These treatments, by supporting the health of the unborn child and expectant mother, attempt to influence early genetic expressions, thereby leading to a healthier next generation. A milk-based regimen can be given to the expectant mother from the first month until delivery.

It is one of my lifelong ambitions to create a centre that supports couples who wish to have children. They will be aided in their desire to become responsible parents right from the outset. The centre will help them prepare to conceive by creating conducive preconditions. They will be aided through pregnancy, delivery and post-natal procedures, and then given comprehensive guidelines to improve the quality of the child's life until the age of twelve. *Prakarayoga* is a day-wise, week-wise, month-wise and year-wise medication regimen to protect the child from any diseases, external and internal. '*Prakara*' means 'wall'—protecting the child by increasing its innate immunity until the age of twelve. Then immunity will be for life (*Arogya Kalpadruma*).

For the rest of one's life, Ayurveda prescribes sustainable healthcare methodologies, including daily and seasonal rituals, occasional cleansing of the body and seasonal changing of food habits.

These methodologies influence gene expression, either stopping the mutation of a disease-causing gene or making it dormant. They can also promote health by activating helpful genes. Let's have a deeper look at these methodologies.

Seasonal Rituals

The six *ritus* (seasons) of the year are *vasantha* (spring), *greeshma* (summer), *varsha* (monsoon), *sharad* (autumn), *hemantha* (winter) and *shishira* (late winter). In each season, we accumulate doṣa imbalances and acquire toxins, and these need to be cleansed at the end of the season. Hence, the need for seasonal rituals.

Based on the above, seasons are classified into two groups—*adana* kāla (period of exhaustion) and *visarga* kāla (period of strength and enrichment). Needless to say, the intensity of each season varies from one geography to another, and we should keep this in mind when practising seasonal rituals. The individual and the acharya both should use their discretion.

Let's have a look at the best practices for the various seasons.

Seasonal Rituals at a Glance: Shishira, Vasantha and Greeshma

	Shishira (Cold, Dewy Season)	**Vasantha (Hot and Dry Season)**	**Greeshma (Intense Hot Season)**
Weather	Cold winds and temperature	• Season of flowers and origin of new leaves • The sun is hot, the wind is dry	• Intense heat with powerful sun rays and unhealthy wind • The river bodies are dry and plants appear lifeless
Predominant Rasa	Tikta	Kaṣāyaka (astringent)	Katu (pungent)
Predominant Pañca Mahābhūta (Element)	Ākāśa (space)	Pṛthvi (earth) and vāyu (air)	Agni (fire) and vāyu (air)
Bala (Strength)	Less	Moderate	Less
Doṣa Dynamic	Accumulation of kapha	Vitiation of kapha	Accumulation of vāta; pacification of kapha

Agni/Anala Digestive Fire	Very high	Low	Low
Impact of Season	• The body needs energy to keep warm • Good time to consume hardy, nutritious food • Not eating enough can harm health through metabolizing of tissues (dhātu) • Fatigue, if dehydrated	Reduced digestive capacity	• Prone to diseases • The body may easily experience dehydration, exhaustion, lethargy
Effects	• Strength-giving • Nourishing to the body • Increased and easy digestion	Prone to diseases	• Drinking alcohol may cause emaciation, debility, burning sensation and delusion • Food restrictions are more
Approach to Food and Food Groups	Prefer the following kinds of food: • Amla (sour), madhura (sweet) and lavana (salty) • Nutritious and heavy • Fatty • High-fibre	Prefer the following kinds of food: • Easily digestible • Moisture-free and fat-free • Tikta, katu and kaṣāyaka	Prefer the following kinds of food: • Easily digestible • Food having madhura (sweet), *snigdha* (unctuous), sheeta (cold) and *drava* (liquid) properties

Best-Suited Foods	• Freshly harvested grains: wheat, millet, maize, gram, split green gram, black gram and lentil, groundnut, corn, sesame seeds and new rice • Root vegetables such as carrot, beetroot, radish • Cabbage, cauliflower, pumpkin, turnip, yam, lettuce, broccoli, garlic • Green vegetables • Sprouts • Freshly made vegetable soups • Carrot halwa • Jaggery • Ginger, garlic • Rabbit, fish, prawn, crab, buffalo, sheep, goat, pig, hen	• Old barley, wheat, rice, green gram • Honey, honey water • Boiled herbal water (*asana,* chandana, *musta*) • Unspoilt fermented beverages such as *aāsava, ariṣṭa, seedhu* • Fermented sugarcane juice, fermented grape juice • Roasted meats such as that of rabbit	• Corn flour mixed with very cold water • Sugar (after taking cold water bath) • Milk with sugar candy (at bedtime) • Cold water kept in mud pots, along with *paatala, karpoora* • A syrup made using *ananta* (hemidesmusindicus), *kamala* (lotus), *gulaba* (rose), *amra* (mango), *draksha* (grapes), chandana (sandal), *ushira* and *jambhira* (lemon), after diluting with water • 1–2 tsp of gulkand with milk to reduce itching, digestive disturbances, gastritis, giddiness and burning sensation in the body, eyes, palms and soles

	• Banana, orange, grapes, kiwi, passion fruit, pear, pomegranate, pomelo, dates, haritaki *(Terminali chebula)*, dry fruits • Sugarcane • Milk and milk products such as clarified butter, khoa, rabri, kheer and cream		• Fresh fruit juices, buttermilk, tender coconut water, juice made of soaked dry grapes, fig and dates • Meat soups • Mango, grapes, pomegranate • Cucumber and carrot salads • Boiled rice • Churned curd with pepper
Food Groups to Be Avoided	• *Laghu* (light) and sheeta (cold) foods • Foods having predominant rasas of katu (pungent), tikta (bitter) and kaṣāyaka (astringent)	• New grains • Curd • Sour, cold drinks • Greasy food with high water content	• Lavana (salty), katu (pungent) and amla (sour) foods • Ushna (warm) foods
Foods to Be Avoided	• Potatoes • Whole grains (any gram), green peas • Light foods and drinks • Cold drinks and cold water • Pungent, bitter and astringent food and drinks • Unhealthy snacking	• Foods that are hard to digest • Those that are sheeta (cold), snigdha (unctuous), guru (heavy), amla (sour) and madhura (sweet) • Milkshakes, curds, alcohol	Spicy, hot, sour, dry food

Best Practices	• Massaging with oil/powder/paste (head and body)
	• Bathing in warm water
	• Consuming hot water
	• Exposure to sunlight
	• Staying hydrated
	• Wearing warm clothes
	• Walking, but not much and without too much exposure to cold winds
	• Avoiding unhealthy snacking
	• Avoiding late nights
		• Bathing with warm water
		• *Udvartana* (dry powder massage) with powder of chandana (santalum album), *kesara* (crocus sativus), *agaru*
		• *Kavala* or *gaṇḍūṣa* (gargle)
		• *Dhooma* (smoking of herbs)
		• *Anjana* (collyrium), and evacuative measures such as vamana and nasya (nasal medications)
		• Exercising
		• Avoid sleeping in the during the day
			• Staying in cool places
			• Applying sandalwood and other aromatic pastes on the body
			• Bathing in cold water
			• Adornment with flowers
			• Wearing light dresses
			• Napping in the daytime
			• Experiencing the moon's rays and night's breeze
			• Keeping surroundings clean
			• Using mosquito nets or fumigating the indoors with the smoke of dried neem leaves in the evenings (unless there are asthma patients)
			• Avoiding:
			  o Excessive exercise and manual labour
			  o Alcohol and excessive sexual activity
			  o Excessive exposure to sunlight

Seasonal Rituals at a Glance: Varsha, Sharad and Hemantha

	Varsha (Monsoon)	**Sharad (Autumn)**	**Hemantha (Winter)**
Weather	• The sky is covered with heavy clouds, rains occur without thunderstorms • Ponds, rivers, etc., are filled with water, which can become impure	• The sun becomes bright, the sky remains clear or dotted with white clouds • The earth is covered with wet mud	• Cold winds and chill • Nights are longer than the day
Predominant Rasa	Amla (sour)	Lavana (salty)	Madhura
Predominant Pañca Mahābhūta (Element)	Pṛthvi (earth) and agni (fire)	Ākāśa (space) and agni (fire)	Pṛthvi (earth) and ākāśa (space)
Bala (Strength)	Less	Moderate	Highest
Doṣa Dynamic	• Vitiation of vāta doṣa • Deposition of pitta doṣa	• Pacification of vitiated vāta doṣa • Vitiation of pitta doṣa	• Pacification of vitiated pitta doṣa

Agni/Anala Digestive Fire	*Vishamagni* (erratic)	Increased	Increased
Impact of Season	• Prone to diseases; immunity is low • All the doṣas get vitiated	Increased digestive capacity	• Appetite increases; can eat well • Immunity is high; less prone to diseases • Strength is higher
Approach to Food and Food Groups	Prefer the following kinds of foods: • Amla (sour) and lavana (salty) foods • Unctuous foods • Warm and fresh foods	Prefer the following kinds of foods: • Madhura (sweet) and tikta (bitter) foods • Light foods • Foods with cold properties • Pitta-pacifying foods • Moisture-free and fat-free foods	Prefer unctuous, madhura (sweet), amla (sour) and lavana (salty) foods
Best-Suited Foods	• Deep well water, medicated and/or boiled • Cereals such as old barley, rice, wheat, etc.	• Old barley, wheat, rice, green gram • Honey, honey water, sugar candy	• New rice, flour preparations, green gram, black gram, freshly harvested corn, etc. • Various meats, fats

	• Soups of meat and pulses, hot and sour soups • Wine prepared from grapes, fermented decoctions • Old buttermilk processed with herbs	• Boiled herbal water (with added asana, chandana, musta)—use *hamsodaka* (water that gets heated by sun rays and gets cooled by moon rays • Unspoilt fermented beverages such as aāsava, ariṣṭa, seedhu • Fermented sugarcane juice, fermented grape juice, *maadhava* • *Patola* (Trichosanthesdiocia) • Flesh of animals of dry land	• Milk and milk products • Sugarcane products, • Fermented preparations, sura (wine) • Sesame
Food Groups to Be Avoided	• Light and cold foods • Foods having predominant katu (pungent), tikta (bitter), kaṣāyaka (astringent) tastes	Hot, bitter, sweet, and astringent foods	• Vāta-aggravating foods • Cold and dry foods
Foods to Be Avoided	• River water • Churned preparations having more water • Wine • Foods that are hard to digest, such as meat	• Curd • Oil • Strong liquors • The meat of aquatic animals	• Spicy, hot, sour, dry food • Cold drinks of any kind

Best Practices	• Bathing in boiled water • Rubbing the body with oil after bath • Medicated *vashti* (enema) • Keeping warm • Exposing clothes to fragrant fumes • Using medicated fragrant fumes to fumigate the indoors • Avoiding: o Excessive walking o Staying on the upper storeys of a house, using medicated fragrant fumes at home o Getting wet in the rain o Sleeping in the daytime o Excessive exercise or manual labour o Excessive sexual activity o Staying at the riverbank	• Spending evenings on terraces of houses • Eating only when hungry • Wearing flower garlands, pearls • Exposure to moon rays in the first three hours of the night • Applying the paste of chandana (sandalwood) on the body • Medical procedures such as virechana (purging), raktamokṣaṇa (bloodletting using leeches), etc. • Avoiding: o Sleeping in the daytime o Excessive exposure to sunlight	• Exercising • Body and head massage • Bathing with warm water • Sunbathing • Exposure to fragrant fumes • Keeping warm with heavy clothing • Sexual indulgence with one partner • Residing in warm homes, preferably with underground chambers

Daily Rituals

Ayurveda provides a list of guidelines for diet, exercise and lifestyle choices. Some of them are mentioned below:

- *Bramhemuhurtheutthishtethi:* Wake up early in the morning, at least one or one-and-a-half hours before sunrise (to do this one should go to bed early and not compromise on the duration of sleep).
    - o If one feels that the food consumed the previous night has not been digested, it is advised to either eat early or sleep until the digestion process is completed.
- *Mala visarjana:* Urinate, clear the bowels as soon as you wake up.
- *Mukhaprakshalana* and *dantadhavana:* Clean teeth, tongue and mouth.
- *Gaṇḍūṣa:* Gargle.
- *Navana:* Self-administer nasal drops.
- *Karnapoorana:* Self-administer oil drops to the ears.
- *Vyayama:* Exercise in accordance with your bala (strength), vaya (age) and ritu (season).
- *Abhyanga:* Apply oil on your body.
- *Snana:* Take a thorough and invigorating bath.
- *Dhyana:* Meditate.
- *Āhāra:* Consume food suited to the prevalent season (see sections below).
- *Sadvritha:* Follow the code of conduct that's apt for your profession, familial roles and station in life.
- *Nidra:* Sleep eight hours or as much as your body needs.

Following these rituals every day will help remove toxins, replenish nutrients, rejuvenate the body and thereby promote health.

Pañca Karma

Along with daily and seasonal rituals, occasional cleansing of the body is also necessary. Pañca karma is perhaps the most important technique available for the complete rejuvenation and cleansing of the body.

Varsha ritu (monsoon) is the best time to start therapeutic Pañca karma for two reasons:

1. The body is going to be enriched.
2. Vāta gets accumulated in this season and this is the best time to remove it.

Contrary to popular belief, pañca karma is not just massage. It is a detailed protocol, not only to treat diseases but also to prevent it from occurring, thereby promoting the well-being of an individual. It also delays the ageing process. Pañca karma eliminates aama from the body—the root cause of illnesses. It also helps in better absorption and digestion of nutrients and medicines, and opens up microchannels that connect tissues.

The five pañca karma procedures are:

1. Vamanạ (therapeutic emesis), or the removal of toxins through the oral route.
2. Virechana (therapeutic purgation), or the removal of toxins through the rectal route.

3. Basti (therapeutic enema), which has been discussed in detail in the chapter 'Gut, GIT and Microbiome'.
4. Nasya (therapeutic nasal drops), or the administering of medicines through the nasal cavities—either through nasal instillation or inhalation of medication.
5. Raktamokṣaṇa (bloodletting), or the extraction of blood from the affected part of the body for healing, usually with the help of *jalauka* (leech) and instruments.

Before pañca karma, the body has to be prepared to accept the treatments. Certain preparatory steps are followed and medicines administered to make the body receptive to the treatment. These are called the *purva* karma treatments. A special set of treatments are conducted after the pañca karma too, and they are called *paschath* karma procedures.

A pañca karma treatment can last a few days or a few weeks and, in exceptional cases, three months. Periodic pañca karma treatment can prevent asthma, allergic rhinitis, obesity and early-onset diabetes.

Purva karma (pre-pañca karma procedures) can include:

- *Deepana and paachana*—oral medicines that are digestive and carminative
- *Snehana* (oleation)
    - o *Abhyanga* (massage with medicated oils)
    - o *Kaya seka* (pouring of medicaments over the body)
- *Snehapana* (internal consumption of several medicated ghee/oils according to disease, in a progressively increasing dose to saturate the body with it. It may extend from four to seven days)
- *Swedana* and *utklesha* (sudation)

- o *Patra pinda sweda* (sudation with fresh medicated herbs)
- o *Cūrṇa pinda sweda* (sudation with medicated powder)
- o *Avagahasweda* (immersion in a tub filled with a decoction of herbs)
- o *Bhashpasweda* (sudation in the steam chamber)

Paschath karma (post pañca karma procedures) can be followed for a period of three to seven days. Since it is not advisable to resume a normal diet immediately after pañca karma, the patient can be taken through a series of steps—the duration and comprehensiveness of these steps will depend on the intensity of the pañca karma procedures. Here are the graded things to be consumed:

- Peya (rice water/thin gruel): Made by adding one part of rice with fourteen parts of water, cooked very well and of very thin consistency.
- Vilepi (thick rice gruel): Thicker than peya. Vilepi is cooked by adding one part of rice to four parts of water. It should contain rice particles.
- Yusha (green gram soup): A form of liquid preparation of grains or pulses—one part of grain/pulse and six parts of water, cooked very well.
- Māṁsa rasa (mutton soup): Thin, nourishing soup made with one part of māṁsa (fresh flesh of goat) cooked very well in eight parts of water.

Mental Health Practices *(Sadvṛttaa)*

No discussion on epigenetics is complete without acknowledging the pivotal role played by the mind in keeping the body healthy.

The sheer discipline and zeal required to practise the methodologies prescribed above stem from our mind, and keeping it healthy requires us to:

- Create an ecosystem that is harmonious and affectionate—this requires family members to move from expectation to acceptance.
- Practise emotional hygiene by sharing your emotional state of mind with those who care. In ancient times, the village ecosystem offered empathetic ears—these could belong to the temple priest, the polite barber, the panchayat elder, elders at home, etc. Today, not all people living in urban areas have such empathy within easy reach. Professional counsellors can fill the void.
- Address the ill effects of negative life experiences—such as bullying, abuse, near-death incidents, involvement in natural or man-made calamities—at the earliest.
- Adhere to time-tested best practices as follows:
    - Speak on the right occasion, using appropriate and pleasant words. Be relevant and brief; don't argue or be untruthful.
    - Give respect to everyone, be it man, woman, child, the elderly or the differently abled.
    - Proactively greet people with a pleasant smile.
    - Be virtuous and compassionate in thought and deed.
    - Neither believe everything and everybody, nor be suspicious.
    - Never insult anybody in public.
    - Tailor your communication according to the nature of the receiver.
    - Treat orphans as you would treat your own children.

- Moderate activities—find the balance between overdoing and abstinence
- Do not gossip, backbite or use abusive language
- Avoid finding fault with others
- Be wary of faithlessness, greed and jealousy
- Look after other people's interests as you would your own

Needless to say, this is just a small glimpse of how we can take care of our mental wellness. Perhaps a later book of mine will do justice to the importance of this subject.

Conclusion

Modern science has recently become enthusiastic about epigenetics. Ayurveda, on the other hand, has been a champion of epigenetics for centuries. Having understood the importance of diet, fitness, the environment and life experiences on health, our ancient acharyas devised mechanisms to maintain the dynamic equilibrium of health.

Ayurveda promises restoration by aiding the expression of helpful genes while making harmful genes dormant. No matter what nature gives us, we can live a healthy life by embracing a nurturing way of life.

7

Pillars of Restoration—Prevention and Promotion*

In September 1978, the International Conference on Primary Health Care was held by the World Health Organization (WHO) in the Kazakh city of Alma-Ata (now Almaty). At a time when most developing countries were struggling to provide basic healthcare to their citizens, this conference made a declaration that was not just ambitious but also innovative.

Instead of focusing on treating diseases alone, the conference identified the following areas as important and deserving of immediate intervention:

- Awareness creation on diseases and treatments
- Food and nutrition
- Water and sanitation
- Family planning, maternal and child care

* Please read this chapter only after reading the previous one titled 'Epigenetics'.

- Immunization
- Prevention of epidemics
- Treatment of disease and availability of drugs

One cannot help but notice that, barring the last one, all the areas listed above are to do with the prevention of diseases and promotion of health. This aligns with the definition of health agreed upon in this conference. According to WHO, '[Health] is a state of complete physical, mental and social wellbeing, and not merely the absence of disease or infirmity, [and] is a fundamental human right.'

The Alma-Ata Declaration went on to observe that sound health was key to leading a socially and financially productive life. So governments, international organizations and societies, in general, were requested to make prevention of diseases and promotion of health an unshakeable way of life by the year 2000.

Today, we can all agree that we, as a species, have lost sight of this target. This has happened in spite of the progress made by allopathy in curbing infectious diseases. Because, even as we conquered microbes, we succumbed to our greed and myopia. We have embraced dysfunctional lifestyles that have made multicausal chronic ailments a widespread phenomenon. We abuse our bodies with foods that are not good for us. We poison our minds with thoughts that create disharmony. Over a period of time, our bodies and minds become pale shadows of their vibrant selves.

One day—hopefully soon—the whole world will realize that Ayurveda can make a great contribution to combating these lifestyle ailments. Indeed, Ayurveda is a holistic way of life that promotes health and prevents diseases. It acknowledges that the body is not static. It has to maintain a dynamic equilibrium; it must change as it ages and as external factors get altered.

We have already discussed a framework for maintaining the body's dynamic equilibrium in the 'Epigenetics' chapter—by which I mean the daily, seasonal and occasional cleansing rituals that help in nurturing and rejuvenating the body. In this chapter, we will extend the framework to understand the impact of our consumption patterns.

Health—the By-Product of a Way of Life

Ayurveda as a way of life is explained in this sloka:

Dharmartha kama mokshanam aarogyam moolamuttamam
Rogaaha tasya apahartaraaha shreyaso jeevitasya cha

—*Charaka Samhitha Sutra Sthana, Chapter 1*

The meaning of this sloka is: Dharma (virtuous acts and moral order), artha (wealth and prosperity), kama (worldly desires, both physical and material) and moksha (heavenly happiness or liberation from the cycles of birth) are the four goals of human life. These can be attained only by a balanced and healthy mind and body. Ayurveda offers guidelines to conquer the imbalance of health, which is essential to attaining the ultimate goal—moksha—and leading a healthy life here.

In order to ascertain whether a physician's help is required, you can make use of fifteen indicators of sound health:

Thad lakshanam pañca dashaprakara -
Aharakanksha swadanam vipaka:
Pureesha Mutranila Srushtatha cha:
Tadendiryaartha grahane cha saktihi:
Manasukhatvam balavarna labha:
Swapna Sukhena Pratibodhanam Cha.

—*Bhaishajya Ratnavali*

Physical Indicators (Non-Sensory)

1. **The desire for food**: You experience hunger three times a day and feel satisfied after every meal.
2. **Effortless digestion**: Everything that is consumed is digested effortlessly, without fatigue or discomfort. You feel light even after eating without restrictions and as per your desires.
3. **Proper bowel movement**: You move your bowels once or twice a day. Consistent stools are passed without distress.
4. **Urination**: Urination causes no irritation, inconvenience, discomfort or burning. There is no increased frequency, turbidity or discolouration.
5. **Gases**: Gases formed during digestion are released without any problem and they are not accompanied by a strong smell or sound.

Physical Indicators (Sensory)

6. **Eyes:** Your eyes function well without external aids such as spectacles.
7. **Ears:** You experience sound hearing without external aid.

8. **Nose:** Your olfactory sense is keen and capable of discerning all types of gross and subtle smells.
9. **Tongue:** You can discern and enjoy all six tastes (as described in the chapter 'Tailor-Made Healthcare') without any challenges.
10. **Skin:** You have a good sense of touch.

Meta Indicators

11. **Peace of mind:** Peace of mind is not only psychological but also physical. Can you close your eyes and forget your body parts and forget the world? Is your body painless? Do you have mental peace? If you do, it is a sign of health.
12. **Strength (Bala):** If your strength is appropriate to your age, body constitution and genetic factors, it's a sign of good health.
13. **Complexion:** A bright, radiant face and glowing skin indicate good health.
14. **Sleep:** Do you fall asleep first and then go to bed? That's a sign that you have no difficulty falling asleep. Sound sleep with no disturbances or dreams is another indicator of health.
15. **Waking up:** Waking up without difficulty, feeling fresh and energized and jumping out of bed in the morning after a relaxed night's sleep is a sign of health.

The Meso Health Phenomenon

If all fifteen indicators show you in good health, does that mean you are completely healthy? Maybe or maybe not. Many of us are in a state of meso health, which is a transition stage between health and disease. While in the olden times, people quickly regained their health by eliminating dysfunctional patterns, that's not the case today. Even if we sincerely pursue health, certain macroeconomic forces throw hurdles in our path. More specifically, here are the two major commercial interests that influence our collective behaviour and drag us down towards disease:

1. Pharma and Commercialism

Our pharmaceutical research projects mainly focus on making our medications stronger instead of making our bodies more resilient. So modern hospitals, instead of being healthcare centres, have become disease-management centres. So when we experience disease, our bodies get bombarded with medication. We return home minus the disease and also minus part of our strength. To put it mildly, our attempts to regain health after an illness leave us weaker.

2. Food and Commercialism

In the past, we knew how to use food as medicine. This way, our eating stayed aligned with our experience of the world at any particular moment. Ayurveda itself prescribes personalized diets to combat diseases. However, the industrialization of food has made this a major challenge. Our food habits are no longer guided by science but by the business interests of the food-processing industry. We consume food that is unseasonable and, very often, lacking in nutrition and with an overdose of chemicals.

Perhaps it's time to take a more detailed look at the commercialization of food.

The Impact of Industrialization of Food

When we process food, we add something to it to change its nature in some way. Previously, with the exception of long-shelf-life food such as pickles, food was processed in our kitchens hours or minutes before it was consumed. Today, a great deal of the food we consume is processed across distance and time. Such foods need not be nutritious, but they must be consumable. In other words, the food needn't be alive with nutrients, but it shouldn't be dead and rotting.

Many things are added to food to prevent decay, and they have the potential to wreak havoc on our bodies and minds. If the epidemic of lifestyle diseases faced by humankind is a murder scene, here are the primary suspects:

Preservatives

Humankind has been using Class I preservatives—which include salt, vinegar, sugar, honey, wood smoke, etc.—for thousands of years. Meat, for instance, would be cured with salt for later consumption. Nature told us the secrets of food preservation, and all was well.

Then we went and invented preservatives. We called them Class II, Class III and Class IV preservatives. In addition to the ill effects of consuming chemical preservatives along with our food, we took to consuming stale food and foods inappropriate for the prevalent season and geography. You could drink watermelon juice in peak winter, never mind your body's shocked response to such consumption.

Industries flourished; our bodies suffered.

The situation is worse in developing countries such as India, where many preservatives that are banned in other countries are used freely.

Nowhere is the incredulity of preserved food more evident than in dairy products. Some brands of curds can last a fortnight. (The smart consumer, of course, chooses the other brand, which will 'go bad' in two days.)

Pesticides

Chemical pesticides helped us achieve food surplus (without, for unconnected reasons, eliminating malnutrition and starvation). Thanks to these pesticides, our vegetables and fruits swelled like diseased glands. We could now eat more. We also began eating food that began eating into our health.

Food Enhancers

We add potassium bromate to enhance bread. This chemical, when cooked, creates bromine. Excess consumption of bromine can suppress the metabolism of iodine. It can also create carcinogens in the body. In fact, most food enhancers seem to be wildly carcinogenic. Some of them can also infect our lungs (for example, diacetyl), our heart (for example, MSG), our kidneys (for example, brilliant blue food dye), our stomach (for example, sodium benzoate), etc.

Hormones

Animals are pumped with hormones so that they yield more milk or meat. We are yet to fully understand the impact of hormones in our food, but as of now, we have reason to suspect that they can cause cancer and interfere with our reproductive system.

Fat-Free Foods

Today, milk can be skimmed and yoghurt de-fattened. Non-dairy products, too, have fat-free versions. In the list of murder suspects, fat was pronounced guilty by the West in the 1960s. Today, the West is finally waking up to its mistake and realizing that, in the interim decades, fat-free food has caused more harm than good—because loads of sugar were added to make cardboard-like food palatable.

Added Sugar and Sweeteners

The irony of processed food is that sugar is added to almost all of them, even unlikely foods such as tender coconut water and mustard sauce! So the more processed food we eat, the more we begin craving sugar without even realizing that's what we are craving.

Sugar is a slow poison, manufactured by the removal of micronutrients from sugarcane. Meanwhile, honey, a time-tested natural sweetener, has become a preservative-laden Trojan horse. Even worse are artificial sweeteners (such as aspartame) that are flagrantly carcinogenic and therefore faster poisons than sugar.

Added sugar in processed food has already created a few generations of consumers that demand instant gratification from their plates. Glucose and fructose have the same effect on them as cocaine—lighting their brains up like Christmas trees, making every day a feasting experience. More often than not, their bodies fail to get rid of the excess sugar—and the next trainload of sweetness arrives sooner than the previous one has been unpacked by their bodies.

In the chapter 'Tailor-Made Healthcare', we learn that madhura-tasting (naturally sweet) foods should be dominant in our diets. That's because staple foods such as rice, wheat and lentils are naturally sweet in their composition due to the presence of glucose. Come to think of it, all our sugar requirements are easily fulfilled while consuming natural and healthy foods. In the pre-industrialized era, sweets were reserved for special occasions and made from wholesome jaggery or honey. By merely returning to that simpler time, we can reclaim our ideal body weight and, perhaps, our health.

Adulterants

The food industry is notorious for adding substances to food that simply do not belong in it. Hence we find urea in milk, melamine in powdered infant formula, titanium dioxide and skimmed milk in cottage cheese (to make them white), bromates in bottled water, calcium carbide in fruits (for ripening them quicker) and arsenic in packaged fish.

Extracts

Fruit juices have the sugar content of five fruits in one typical serving and zero fibre content. Consuming this puts stress on one's guts. Added preservatives, sugar, adulterants and colour add to the list of problems.

Is it any wonder that consuming processed food accumulates aama in our bodies? So Ayurveda will tell you what you already know—eat as little or no processed food, stay as close as possible to the origin of the food (by cutting off middlemen) and know your food suppliers as well as you can (which means you can buy your meat and milk from the local butcher and milkman). We need a disclaimer here: Our urban cows are allowed to roam free on our streets so that they can forage in our garbage dumps, so when I say you must know your milkman, I mean you must know how he treats his cattle.

What Foods to Consume

From the very beginning, we've been promoting the magnanimity of nature. Quite obviously, we need to consume what's natural. Let's dispel a few myths here:

Organic Is Not the Same as Natural

Processed organic food is still processed food and not necessarily nutritious.

Vegan is Not Synonymous with Healthy

Ayurveda relies on dairy products to provide much-needed nutrition to the human body. Nowhere is this more evident than in the fact that a newborn is given a drop of ghee before its first taste of mother's milk. It stands to reason that Ayurveda does not see the point in prescribing a dairy-free diet to one and all. Modern studies suggest that a vegan diet can cause vitamin B12 deficiency—B12 is a micronutrient that's produced neither by the human body nor the cattle humans consume. It is found in trace amounts in the soil that the cattle consumes while chewing grass.

It is also important to note that it is possible to gorge on all kinds of unhealthy, calorific vegan foods. While we have reason to admire the tenacity and willpower of vegans, not all their practices are health-conscious.

Non-Vegetarianism Is Not Necessarily a Path to Doom

In the 'Introduction' itself, I have stated that there is no need to create a false equivalence between Ayurveda and vegetarianism. Ayurveda willingly looks at some meats as sātmya to those who are used to it and will recommend a diet inclusive of wholesome, unprocessed meat to those who consume it regularly.

Instead of making any food forbidden, Ayurveda talks about moderation and the modus operandi of consumption. After all, everything is potentially helpful or potentially harmful. Ayurveda's open-mindedness is evident nowhere more than its approach to the consumption of alcohol.

There is no doubt that regular consumption of alcohol can weaken the body and affect our internal organs. So while not recommending alcohol, Ayurveda suggests a holistic approach to alcohol consumption—one that asks the consumer to prepare the body, mind and soul for alcohol. Specifically, the consumer should:

- Take care of hygiene (perhaps by bathing) and wear clean clothes, jewels, garlands and perfumes.
- Offer prayer and touch auspicious objects.
- Find a setting that's cool and surrounded by trees that are shedding one's favourite flowers.
- Have comfortable seating and reclining furniture.

- Be served alcohol in a vessel made of a noble metal, perhaps studded with jewels.
- Consume green salads, fruits, roasted meat, etc. simultaneously.
- Precede alcohol consumption with rituals appropriate to their prakṛti.
- Be in the company of friends who have satvik or rajasik dispositions and avoid those with tamasik personalities. Pleasant talkers, artistically talented, empathetic people and best friends are preferred.

Let's ignore the hyperboles of the rituals. Let's do away with those rituals that are obsolete or impractical. Let's just focus on the core message here—that a substance as potentially harmful as alcohol will also have minimal or no impact on our bodies if we associate this consumption with positivity. In short, alcohol should generate happiness, energy, nourishment, good health, virility and pleasant intoxication. It should also increase appetite, promote voice and complexion, increase strength and remove fear, grief and fatigue.

Conclusion

We don't have to revert to an earlier era to be healthy. We just have to bring the goodness of that era to our times while also eliminating the unnecessary trappings. So processed food need not play any role in our lives.

Ayurveda focuses more on *how* something is consumed rather than *what*. Sugar can be consumed by chewing sugarcane. Alcohol can be consumed in a happy atmosphere.

Taking care of our consumption patterns will contribute greatly to the prevention of diseases and promotion of health. Our bodies are designed to restore themselves to their best avatars if only we give them a chance to do so.

8

Tailor-Made Healthcare

At this very moment, somewhere on our planet, a woman is being diagnosed with breast cancer. She will have to undergo surgery, radiation and/or chemotherapy. After that, she will be given a particular drug that can potentially avoid a relapse of her cancer. With hope and trepidation, she begins taking the drug. In this particular woman's case, it will later emerge that her body cannot metabolize this drug. By the time she and her doctors realize this, valuable time would have been wasted.

It emerges that our DNA plays a huge role in how medicines are metabolized by our bodies. Some of us might metabolize a medicine quicker than we should, some others might metabolize it slower than desirable and a few of us might be lucky enough to experience optimal metabolization of the medicine. The truly unfortunate are like the woman described above—they belong to the fourth category of people who simply cannot metabolize the medicine at all.

Knowing the link between DNA and the effect of medicines has given rise to what is perhaps the most exciting field in modern medicine—pharmacogenomics, also referred to as tailor-made medicines or personalized medicine.

The term means as it sounds. It is about creating medicines that cater to people fitting into a particular genetic profile. So in the future, the woman described above will be given medicines that are guaranteed to be metabolized by her body—because she will be given a variation of the medicine suitable for her individual genetic profile.

The human genome project has accelerated the advent of pharmacogenomics. Pharmaceutical companies have now started making genetic mapping/genome scanning accessible to individuals. With each individual that is scanned and mapped, the database gets that much richer. So researchers have more test data at their disposal, which means that research findings can become more accurate and more widely applicable.

As of today, cancer, diabetes and dementia are at the forefront of pharmacogenomic research, since genes and epigenetics have such a strong bearing on these diseases.

In the long run, modern research will help Ayurveda physicians offer a greater degree of tailor-made healthcare. Having said that, it is important to note that Ayurveda has offered tailor-made healthcare since time immemorial.

Ayurveda and Pharmacogenomics

Ayurveda has always maintained that there is no one healthcare procedure that fits everybody's needs. So it recommends that the patient be seen as a whole (covered in the chapter 'The Whole Plant, the Whole Person'). Additionally, we have already seen that Ayurveda creates a distinct profile for each individual based on ten factors—some of these factors allude to their body type, some to environmental factors and others to their lifestyle and/or current life situation.

To get a glimpse of how these ten factors result in tailor-made healthcare, let's take a case study. In a single calendar year, two women of almost the same age approached me with the same primary grievance that they had experienced for the same duration. My treatment approaches to them were drastically different, as is evident from the table below.

	Case 1	Case 2
Gender	Female	Female
Profile Details (Details of ten factors Ayurveda uses to tailor healthcare)		
Vaya (Age)	Madhyama (42 years)	Madhyama (38 years)
Bhoomi Deśa (Type of Geography)	Anūpa (Resident of Austin, Texas, USA)	Sadharana (Resident of Bangalore, India)
Āhāra (Staple Diet)	Rice, wheat, oats	South-Indian (rice-intensive) non-vegetarian food
Doṣa, Dūṣya, Mala (the Functional Units of the Body)	Vāta and kapha doṣa Rasa (plasma) Rakta (blood) Asthi (bone) Māṁsa (muscle)	Vāta and kapha doṣa Rasa (plasma) Rakta (blood) Asthi (bone) Māṁsa (muscle)
Bala (Strength)	Avara (Low body strength)	Madhyama (Medium body strength)

Kāla (Season)	Sharad (treatment began in autumn)	Greeshma (treatment began in summer)
Anala (Digestive Strength)	Mandāgni (Low digestive fire)	Mandāgni (Low digestive fire)
Prakṛti (Constitutional Type)	Kapha–pitta	Kapha–vāta
Satva (Threshold for Pain)	Madhyama (Moderate)	Madhyama (Moderate)
Sātmya (Well-Entrenched Habits)	Regular exercise and measured food consumption	No exercise regimen followed

Diagnostic Details

Major Grievance	Cervical spondylosis for 1 year	Cervical spondylosis for 1 year
Symptom(s)	• Pain in the neck radiating into the right hand • Accompanied by difficulty in the movement of the right shoulder	• Pain in the neck radiating to the right hand • Accompanied by: o Burning sensation in the tips of fingers o Swelling and stiffness in the finger joints o Numbness of both hands, with the right hand being more affected

Secondary Grievance(s)	• Pollen allergy • Frequent sinusitis with frequent nose blocks	• Increased blood cholesterol • Frequent bloated abdomen • Acidity
Process of Diagnosis	Blood and MRI investigations	MRI of the cervical spine, which revealed C5-C6 osteophytes, and diagnosed as cervical spondylosis
Divergent Treatment Models		
Although secondary grievances vary and this differentiated the treatment to some extent, the main reason for differentiated treatments was their unique individual profiles.		
Treatments	Inpatient: 3 weeks	Inpatient: 0 days
	OPD: 1 year	OPD: 3 months
	Full body massage	Full body massage
	Bolus fomentation using herbal leaves, powders and oil	Bolus fomentation using herbal leaves, powders and oil
	Warm oil pack on the vertex	Warm oil pack on the vertex
	Herbal paste application on the neck and thoracic region	Pouring of warm, fermented, medicated water on the body
	Warm oil pack on the cervical region	Oral medication
	Therapeutic purgation	
	Cleansing and nourishing enema	

	A special type of massage on vital points of the body	
	Medicated oil instillation into the nostrils	
	Special treatment with medicated milk and rice bolus fomentation	
	Yoga and meditation	

The woman from Texas had to undergo three weeks of inpatient care, where she was administered many more care methodologies, partly because the kāla and deśa components aggravated her secondary grievances. Her OPD treatment, too, lasted four times longer than that of the woman from Bangalore.

Just as allopathic doctors have their diagnostic tools, Ayurveda uses the ten profile factors of a patient to come up with drastically different approaches to treatment. Let's understand each of these ten in detail.

Ayurveda's Ten Factors

Dūṣya (Structural Units of the Body)

There are seven structural tissues in the body: rasa (plasma), rakta (blood), māṁsa (muscle), medās (fat), asthi (bone), majjā (marrow/nerve) and shukra (reproductive tissue). The dūṣya factor examines the damage to these tissues caused by a disease. In diabetes, for example, rasa, rakta, māṁsa and medās are damaged.

Dūṣya and the Tailor-Made Approach

An Ayurveda physician will know which tissues get damaged in each disease. This helps in the creation of an appropriate treatment plan.

Deśa (Geography)

Deśa can allude to one of two things: the geographical location of the patient or the affected body part of the patient. Here, we will consider the geographical location, which can be of three types: *anūpa* deśa, *jangala* deśa and *sadharana* deśa.

	Anūpa Deśa	*Jangala Deśa*	*Sadharana Deśa*
Predominant Prakṛti in the Geography	Kapha	Vāta	Places that have a balanced combination of vāta, pitta and kapha
Kind of Landscape	River basins and water-clogged areas	• Dry and rocky, few rivers and few trees • Landscapes such as hill stations	Neither hilly nor marshy
Suitable for	Vāta-dominant people with lean body structures	Kapha-pitta predominant people	Generally recommended for all
Unsuitable for	E.g.: Diabetic people	E.g.: People with skin diseases	None

Pitta-prominent places are uninhabitable and hence are not a part of this list.

Deśa and the Tailor-Made Approach

In the past, Ayurveda mainly used medicinal resources that were available locally. Ayurveda believes that a person's body is more responsive to medicines that are sourced locally. Hence, medicines can be personalized based on the geographical location of the patient and available flora and fauna, etc.

Geographical location can also be connected with bala and sātmya.

Bala (Strength)

Bala alludes to the physical strength required to handle the medicines ingested into one's system. There are three types of balas:

i. ***Sahaja bala***

This is the bala a person is born with, which varies according to demography as well as according to individuals of each demography. People from Africa are expected to be strong. In India, people from Punjab are expected to have higher sahaja bala as compared to people from Karnataka.

ii. ***Kālājā bala***

This has two meanings:

a) *Seasonal strength*: Refers to the variation in one's strength during different seasons. During the adana seasons, which are generally a time of weakening, one has to be careful with medicines. On the other hand, visarga kāla enhances one's strength, thereby allowing the physician to prescribe strong medicines. This is discussed further in the kāla sub-section.

b) *Strength based on the age of the patient*: A child or an old person is expected to have less strength than a young adult. This is further discussed in the *vaya* sub-section below.

iii. ***Yuktikruta bala***

This is the bala acquired with the help of substances such as *chyavanprash* or rasāyana concoctions. A physician needs to know what substances are already being consumed in order to determine the dosage and potency of the medicines to be prescribed.

For each of these three types of balas, the ability of the individual to handle medicines can be pravara (high), madhyam (medium) or avara (low).

Bala and the Tailor-Made Approach

A pravara bala patient can handle the maximum dosage of medicine, whereas the physician will lower the potency and/or dosage if the patient has madhyam or avara bala.

Kāla (Season)

Kālam/kāla refers to seasons that influence the ecosystem occupied by the patient at the time of diagnosis. The term 'kāla' can also be used to refer to the six stages of an ailment (discussed in detail in the chapter 'Pathogenesis and the Path of Moderation').

We have already looked at the various kālas in the chapter 'Epigenetics'. Here is a quick look at the table:

Adana Kāla (Period of Exhaustion)	Visarga Kāla (Period of Strength and Enrichment)
Shishira (Post winter)	Varsha (Monsoon)
Vasantha (Spring)	Sharad (Autumn)
Greeshma (Summer)	Hemantha (winter)

Kāla and the Tailor-Made Approach

Since seasons influence our body strength, they indirectly influence how medicines work on us. Again, the physician modulates potency and/or dosage. We have already covered in detail how to adapt to each season in the chapter 'Epigenetics'.

Anala (Digestive Fire)

Anala or *analam* refers to the digestive fire (power) in a person. Again, digestive fire varies greatly from one person to another, which impacts the potency and/or dosage of medicines administered.

There are three types of anala: *teekshna agni*, *mandāgni* and *vishama agni*, with *samagni* being the balanced one.

	Vishama Agni	*Teekshna Agni*	*Mandāgni*	*Samagni*
Intensity of Digestive Fire (Anala)	Alternating/ Variable	High/Strong	Low/Weak	Medium
Impact on Treatment	• Sometimes behaves like teekshna agni, and sometimes like *mandāgni*	• The strongest of medicines with the highest of potencies can be administered • Person's digestive fire often compared with a furnace	A physician will either give medicines to enhance the digestive fire or reduce the potency and/or dosage of the medicine	Medicines of moderate potency administered

Analam also influences koshta behaviour and bowel movements.

Anala and the Tailor-Made Approach

When the digestive fire of a patient is low, the physician gives medicines of lower potency and/or dosage. Or the physician can enhance the patient's digestive fire using a sophisticated process of 'rebooting' the stomach as follows:

1. The patient is asked to consume ghee for a specified number of days.

2. The patient is then asked to consume a prescribed diet for a couple of days—along with massages.
3. A strong purgative is administered the next day. This eliminates accumulated aama, which was the cause of the low digestive fire.
4. Now, the digestive fire is rekindled, just as one starts a campfire. The campfire is first fed cotton, then dry leaves, then twigs and, once it starts burning with gusto, pieces of log and wood are added. Similarly, small portions of easily digestible foods are given before the diet is made heavier.

Prakṛti (Constitutional Type)

We have discussed the seven prakṛti types in the chapter 'Prakṛti and Gene-Mapping', where we established beyond doubt that prakṛti has a strong linkage with specific gene markers. By understanding prakṛti, you can choose better where you live, what you eat, etc.

Here are some important characteristics of each prakṛti:

Vāta	**Pitta**	**Kapha**
• Constipation • Lean body type • High/low—undecided appetite • Body cramps • Reduced sleep	• Fast digestion • Disturbed and lot of REM sleep • Warm and reddish body • Skin blemishes	• Slow or ordinary digestion • Bulky and stout • Well-formed joints • Excessive sleep

Prakṛti and the Tailor-Made Approach

Prakṛti has a great say in tailoring the treatment by indirectly influencing other factors:

- Prakṛti influences dietary considerations, which are part of the treatment. Details are given in the sub-section titled 'Āhāra' below.
- Prakṛti influences analam, the digestive fire, which, in turn, impacts potency and/or dosage.
- Prakṛti also positively or negatively influences health, based on the deśam (geography) in which the person is located.

Vaya (Age)

Vaya or age of a human being can be broadly categorized as *baalyam* (childhood), *youvanam* (young adulthood), *madhyamam* (middle age) and *vardhkyam* (old age).

	***Baalyam* (Childhood)**	***Youvanam* (Youth)**	***Madhyamam* (Middle Age)**	***Vardhkyam* (Old Age)**
Age Range	0 to 16	17 to 31	32 to 70	71+
Dominant *Prakṛti*	Kapha	Kapha	Pitta	Vāta
Approach to Treatment	• Kapha-pacifying medicines • All medicines in mild paediatric dosages	• Pitta-pacifying medicines • Medicines of high potency and/or dosages administered, assuming age-appropriate bala	• Same as youvanam, unless other factors make us reconsider how we treat the person	• Vāta-pacifying medicines • Medicine potency and/or dosages reduced

	• Certain pañca karma procedures cannot be performed	• Usually possible to conduct complicated healthcare procedures		• Certain pañca karma procedures cannot be performed

Vaya and the Tailor-Made Approach

From the above table, it is evident that the entire spectrum of medicines and procedures is not available to baalya and vruddha patients. The physician will tread carefully when addressing patients in these two age groups.

Satvam (Pain Threshold)

In simplified terms, satvam or satva refers to a patient's pain threshold. While some of us are capable of bearing extreme pain, others may faint at the mere sight of blood. However, satvam has a broader definition.

It is a psychiatric assessment of the individual. During the assessment, we get to know about the patient and their emotional response to the illness. Some patients seek extreme attention while others manage with fortitude. Ayurveda believes in treating the patient as a whole. So the treatment must cater to both mind and body.

Satvam is classified as below:

i. ***Pravara (high) satvam***
A person with pravara satvam can be started off with high dosage and potency medicines. S/he can undergo all forms of treatments. Such a person is called 'satvavan'—the fearless experiencer of adversity.

ii. ***Hīna or avara (low) satvam***
A hīna satvam person will experience a more cautious approach to treatment.

Satvam and the Tailor-Made Approach

An *Ayurveda* physician will not prescribe certain procedures to people of avara or hīna (low) satvam. These include:

- Bloodletting—with the help of jalauka (leech)
- Vamana or medicinal emesis

Avara satvam people are usually given only pacifying medicines.

Sātmya (Habits)

Sātmya refers to habits one's body is used to. Here are a couple of areas that we allude to while talking about sātmya:

i. **Food**
Our bodies get used to a certain diet, and we may not be able to switch to a new staple grain or a new diet overnight. For instance:

- Some of us must consume non-vegetarian food in every meal, whereas others may not be able to consume even one bite of it.
- Rice eaters might find it challenging to switch to wheat or barley. Those not used to ragi might find it difficult to digest it all of a sudden.

ii. **Alcohol, smoking and other addictive substances**
Ayurveda encourages all good sātmyas and suggests quitting unhealthy sātmyas when necessary. However, care must be taken about other factors, such as the age of the patient.

Take, for instance, an eighty-five-year-old man who had been chewing tobacco for several decades. His son insisted that he quit his addiction. He reluctantly quit the habit in one go. Within no time, he went into depression and died a year later.

Sātmya and the Tailor-Made Approach

An Ayurveda physician will ask an extensive range of questions to know what is *sātmyam*, or habitual to a patient. Good sātmyas will be encouraged, and exit options will be identified for bad sātmyams. However, the physician will keep in mind other factors of the person (especially bala, analam and vaya) while recommending that the patient quit a bad sātmyam. More often than not, a tapered approach is recommended.

- For example, diabetics who are addicted to alcohol suffer a lot. However, stopping consumption of alcohol at once may lead to depression, bodily discomfort and other problems. Gradually altering the sātmyam, on the other hand, can produce desirable results.

- Similarly, an Ayurveda physician will not recommend an overnight implementation of a new diet, nor will he recommend changing the diet too often.
- As mentioned in the chapter 'Gut, GIT and Microbiome', even our intolerance to a certain food group such as lactose or gluten can be rectified by using a gradual and patient process.

Āhāra (Food)

A person who understands food has a greater chance of staying healthy. Underconsumption, overconsumption and/or inappropriate consumption of food lead to ill health. Nutrition experts today suggest understanding food by fibre content, starch, sugar content, carbohydrates, protein, etc. However, Ayurveda understands food through taste, which leads to six types of food categories: madhura (sweet), amla (sour), lavana (salt), tikta (bitter), ooshna (spicy) and kaṣāyaka (astringent).

	Madhura (Sweet)	**Amla (Sour)**	**Lavana (Salty)**	**Tikta (Bitter)**	**Ooshna (Katu) (Spicy)**	**Kaṣāyaka (Astringent)**
Strength Ranking	1 (Strongest)	2	3	4	5	6 (Weakest)
Important Considerations	• Should be the dominant food group in the diet • Starch- and fibre-dominant	• In large quantities, will increase kapha and pitta	• Can actuate your *agni* (digestive fire) and increase the speed of metabolism • Excessive consumption quickly leads to health issues	• Increases appetite	• Increases pitta	• Increases Pitta and vāta • Can actuate agni (digestive fire) and increase the speed of metabolism
Food Examples	• Grains • Pulses • Ghee	• Tamarind • Gooseberry • Citrus fruits	• Rock salt • Black salt • Common salt	• Bitter gourd • Ivy gourd • Neem leaves • Fenugreek	• Chilli • Pepper	• Vinegar • Asafoetida (hing) • Cumin seeds • All decoctions

Most Suitable for	• Vāta people			• Kapha people • Obese people and diabetics (unless of vāta prakṛti)	• Kapha people	• Kapha people
Least Suitable for		• Kapha and pitta people	• Kapha people • People prone to high blood pressure and heart diseases	• Vāta people • People with protein deficiency • Thin people	• People with IBS (irritable bowel syndrome) • Kapha people	• Pitta and vāta people

It is interesting to note that whereas the English language uses the same word (hot) to allude to food that is spicy as well as food of high temperature, the Sanskrit language uses similar sounding words. The word for spicy is 'ooshna' and the word for hot is 'uṣṇa' or 'ushna'.

Aaharam (Āhāra) and the Tailor-Made Approach

Food can be medicine or poison, depending on who is consuming what. By understanding other factors (especially prakṛti), an Ayurveda physician can make apt diet recommendations.

Hence, no qualified Ayurveda physician will recommend bitter gourd juice to diabetic patients of the vāta prakṛti. The same juice works wonderfully for diabetics of other prakṛti, but can, in the worst case scenario, be fatal to diabetics of the vāta prakṛti.

Reaffirming the Learning

Now that we have had a substantial look at all ten factors, let us recap our learning by listing out what needs to be done for a person suffering from diabetes.

Diabetes and Ten Factors at a Glance	
Factor	**What to Do**
Dūṣya (Structural Tissues)	Correct the rasa, medās and all the jaleeya dhātu (liquid tissues) using medications and a nutritious and balanced diet. The affected entities in Prameha are vāta, pitta, kapha, rasa, rakta, māṁsa, medas, majja, shukra, mutra and sweda.

Deśa (Geographical Location)	• Shift from marshy places to temperate places. • Food and lifestyle needs to be modified according to the doṣa and the disease one is suffering from.
Bala (Strength)	• For a young person or a person with pravara bala, administer high-potency medicine. OR • Administer rasāyana medicines to increase strength.
Kāla (Season)	• In strength-giving season, administer maximum dosage of high-potency medicine to a young person. • In strength-sapping season, administer medicines of lower potency and/or dosage, unless the person has high bala.
Anala (Digestive Fire)	• If low, administer medicines to increase digestive fire such as *trikatu, ashtachoorna* and sometimes, *ardrakāsavam*.
Prakṛti (Constitution)	• For vāta people, use ghee-based medicine to increase bulk. Use medical enema and oil massage. For kapha people, administer medicines to reduce fat, increase digestion and increase fire in tissues. Also offer vamana and decoction massage.
Vaya (Age)	• Low dosage of medicines for baalya (age 0-16 years) and vruddha (age 71 years and above). • High dosage of medicines for people between the ages of 17 and 70 years.
Satva (Tolerance)	• High—use medical emesis to remove vitiated kapha • Low—use only pacifying medicine.
Satmyam (Habits)	• Young people should quit addictions at a faster rate • Old people can take more time to quit. • People above the age of 70 might have undesirable repercussions on body and mind upon quitting. An extremely cautious and watchful approach is recommended.
Āhāra (Food)	• Gradually shift to low-glycaemic grains (unpolished rice, whole wheat, ragi, etc.). • Use bitter gourd juice if the patient is not of the vāta prakṛti. • Use discretion while making any diet changes.

Conclusion

The ten factors that make up a person's profile together determine every aspect of the health of that person. Ayurveda has always used these ten factors to accurately diagnose a patient and thereby offer personalized healthcare.

Today, modern science is heading in the same direction. Ayurveda can no doubt benefit from the major advances made in pharmacogenomics. At the same time, open-minded Western scientists can benefit from Ayurveda's time-tested pharmacogenomic approaches.

It is high time modern medicine and ancient wisdom came together to offer what our patients need the most—true restoration of body and mind.

9

Limitations of Ayurveda

In April 2015, a sixty-four-year-old woman in Wisconsin, USA, was admitted with heavy lead poisoning. After eliminating all other possible causes of lead toxicity, the local health department identified two Ayurveda medicines as the source of the excess lead swimming in the woman's bloodstream.

For the better part of two decades, Western countries have been dealing with the ill effects of mass-produced Ayurveda medicines. As people in the West get drawn to the holistic model of healthcare that Ayurveda offers, in rare cases, they also become unwitting victims of dubiously manufactured medicines, most of which originate in India.

I myself have mixed feelings about the industrialization of Ayurveda. On the one hand, if we aspire to spread this beautiful science to the far corners of the world, we must have a higher scale of operation. After all, it's no longer possible to source all the required raw materials locally, and industrialization is the solution here. On the other hand, we don't want unhealthy concoctions—designed for pure profit-making—to sully the good name of Ayurveda. Comprehensive regulation to verify the authenticity of Ayurvedic medicines is the need of the hour.

Meanwhile, I still make a great number of medicines myself. I also rely on a few trusted brands to deliver quality medication. These include Zandu, Dhoothapapeshwar, Arya Vaidya Pharmacy (Coimbatore) and Arya Vaidya Shala (Kottakal)—and no, I have not been paid to endorse them.

While industrialization is a challenge that can pose limitations, an honest Ayurveda practitioner must concede that his field of work certainly poses many pure limitations. Let's look at each one in turn:

Ayurveda Is Still an Unexplored Science

Statistical records point out that India houses nearly 1,00,000 medical manuscripts in libraries across the country, out of which a meagre 200–250 manuscripts have actually been read, assimilated and published, partly because a great many manuscripts are nearly impossible to access or retrieve. Some of the best works appear to have been shipped out to be displayed in museums outside India. Who knows what gems of knowledge are losing their sparkle in those untouched manuscripts? Meanwhile, long-dead master physicians might have bequeathed their knowledge to their families, and these manuscripts might be accumulating dust in lofts in households across India.

It is time for researchers and scientists to take an active hand in locating and studying all such manuscripts. Perhaps the key to reviving and transforming healthcare lies in our untold past.

We've Lost Plants and Medicines!

Certain names and descriptions of plants referenced in Ayurveda texts are extremely difficult or impossible to identify today. Some of these plants are extinct, others may have been lost—and without comprehensive pictures, we have no idea of knowing whether the lost plant has been 'found' under another name.

Another limiting factor has been the tenuous connection between plant names in Ayurveda and their botanical equivalents. At times, Ayurveda uses the same name for two different plants, partly because it categorizes plants based on their characteristics, qualities and effects on human beings. For example, *brahmi* is the name for *Centella asiatica* as well as *Bacopa monnieri*. This dual identity causes confusion and ambiguity. In such cases, the modern practitioner cannot be certain about which plant is to be used while making a particular medicine.

Lack of access to essential ingredients is making it impossible to manufacture some of these medicines, which means these potential cures are no longer available. As a consequence, the ambition to provide Ayurvedic painkillers has fallen by the wayside. Texts suggest using medicines such as *mrutasanjeevini* and *marjaramardini*, but practitioners struggle to identify the plants that need to be used in their composition.

Lack of Standardization

Modern medical science is precise in its research methodologies and practice of medicine. There are clearly defined protocols for every step and every situation. This offers a consistent and reliable user experience—less dependent on the physician's skill and expertise.

In contrast, Ayurveda relies on the physician to deliver an error-free healthcare experience.

The challenge is to retain Ayurveda's tailor-made approach while coming up with standardized processes. In other words, it would be great if all Ayurveda physicians accepted a standardized framework of ideas and practices.

Additionally, it's worth noting that any sound scientific endeavour acknowledges its own deficiencies. That's why Ayurveda acknowledges the lack of standardized protocols for certain acute conditions and recommends allopathy in such cases (more on this in the sub-sections below).

Lack of Research

As of now, we have acknowledged that Ayurveda remains unexplored, is bleeding knowledge every passing day and has not been able to convert knowledge into standardized practices.

What's the one idea that can address all three areas? Research. Sound, extensive studies. We need to study thousands of plant species and hundreds of diseases—such as cancer, AIDS and tuberculosis—by leveraging modern technology.

The research will also provide enhanced credibility to Ayurveda. Practitioners of Ayurveda can submit data from case histories so that symptoms, patient profiles, diagnoses, treatment and results are mapped. These, however, are considered circumstantial evidence or C-level proof that a particular methodology/medicine works. Modern science does not accord these findings the respect it reserves for studies conducted using double-blind tests. It's time Ayurveda passed the rigorous tests imposed by such studies, and I have no doubt that, more often than not, Ayurveda will succeed in these tests.

Perhaps the biggest impediment to research is government support in the form of funds, establishment of research institutions, formation of research ethics bodies and formulation of Ayurveda-friendly policies.

Fake Practitioners

While talking about credibility, one cannot ignore the immense damage inflicted by an unchecked army of fake Ayurveda practitioners. These quacks are to be found in every corner. They convert a scientific framework known for its patience into a dangerous scam that promises quick-fixes.

Once a patient has doled out exorbitant fees for miracle cures that are doomed to fail, they understandably decide that all of Ayurveda is a scam, a mirage.

These quacks impact the credibility of local healing traditions too, which, like Ayurveda, must be practised responsibly and knowledgeably.

Questionable Medicines

Ayurvedic medicines are not approved by the FDA in the USA. When manufactured without care, it might contain unacceptable levels of metal content. There have been reports of patients suffering from high levels of lead and arsenic levels after consuming Ayurveda medicine. Side-effects of such consumption include anaemia, fatigue and shortness of breath.

Such episodes dilute the brand of Ayurveda and its true practitioners. The only way out is to make manufacturers of Ayurveda medicines more accountable.

The Professional Commitment of Physicians

My commitment to the science encourages me to accept a large number of complicated cases, where each needs immense personal care and attention. It's not a one-time effort—I need to continue to customize the treatment protocol for each patient, every day, based on what is going on in his/her body.

This is not easy.

The truly individualized treatment model of Ayurveda means that great effort goes into the care of each patient, even when the case is reasonably straightforward. An Ayurvedic physician's capacity to take on more patients is, therefore, limited. Every challenging case demands a commitment that's higher than in allopathy. Not every doctor is prepared to make that level of commitment.

Perhaps this is also a good time to mention the dearth of qualified nursing staff. Ayurveda establishments rely on trained allopathic nurses. This means we have to spend considerable effort in training the nurses in a radically different approach to healthcare.

Ailments Ayurveda Is Legally Not Allowed to Treat

Ayurveda understands that some diseases will vanish over a period of time and be replaced by diseases caused by newer pathogens and emerging dysfunctional lifestyles. The diktat given to practitioners is: 'Do not worry about the name of the disease, look at the doṣa imbalance to understand the disease. Use empirical evidence to treat.'

However, by law, Ayurveda physicians in India are not allowed to treat certain conditions and ailments. Chief among them are:

- Snakebites
- Dog bites
- Malaria
- Tuberculosis (TB)
- HIV
- Leprosy
- Cholera
- Gastroenteritis

Those suffering from the conditions listed above must be attended by an allopathic physician and strictly given state-prescribed drugs. Even if such a drug is known to have side-effects, the word of the law must be followed. Take, for instance, the multi-drug therapy used for TB—it can leave the patient feeling extremely weak. Ayurveda offers rasāyana and *sanjeevanam* to strengthen the patient's body, helping them sustain the enervating effect of multi-drug therapy.

Clearly, Ayurveda has a role to play in offering holistic restoration as a seamless extension to allopathic treatment. However, regulations and legislations prevent us from working on such diseases.

Ailments Ayurveda Will Not Treat

Ayurveda groups diseases into:

- *Sukha sadhya* (easily curable)
- *Kṛcchra sadhya* (difficult to cure)
- *Yapya* (palliative care, mere management of symptoms)
- *Anupakrama* (non-treatable)

Ayurveda considers patients in the last-named category as non-treatable. This rationale may be explained by the example of a patient who has had diabetes for over ten years and has been taking insulin. If his pancreas has stopped producing insulin and has no beta cells, there is nothing left for Ayurveda to restore.

Legal Hurdles in the Availability of Medicine

Raw materials that are essential in the composition of Ayurvedic medicines are sometimes impossible to procure, owing to government rules and regulations.

Plant extracts such as marijuana, opium, stem of sandalwood and animal extracts such as the musk of deer, feather of peacock, horns of deer and claws of some animals—all of which have medicinal properties—cannot be used by law. While poppy seeds are sold everywhere as food and opioids can be prescribed by allopathic doctors, pure opium (obtained from the unripe pods of the same seed) cannot be used even for proven medical purposes.

Ayurveda has mastered the art of harvesting animal extracts without harming the animal or not extracting until the animal has died of natural causes. But regulation is a hurdle that cannot be sidestepped. Ayurvedic practitioners are compelled to look for herbal and other alternatives as poor substitutes.

Allopathic Interventions May Be Sought in Some Areas

There are certain conditions for which consultation with an allopathic physician is recommended by their Ayurvedic counterparts. For instance, in cases of:

- Haemorrhagic conditions
- High blood pressure

- High temperature
- Infectious diseases
- Accidents
- Severe dehydration
- Stroke
- Early-stage blood clots
- Asthma (acute)

Allopathy offers superior emergency care. More specifically in:

- Acute conditions that require a blood transfusion, intravenous intervention or surgery that mandates sterilized conditions and anaesthesia.
- Accident cases that need surgery and blood transfusion.

By incorporating cutting-edge technologies, standardized protocols and the latest research findings, allopathy has left Ayurveda far behind in emergency care. The same can be said for surgery. While Ayurveda has made little or no progress in cutting-edge surgical procedures since the era of Sushruta, the master surgeon, allopathy has grown by leaps and bounds in this area.

Allopathy also has the upper hand in treating infectious diseases, notwithstanding the impact of antibiotics on society. The current approach of creating more intense generations of antibiotics can cause long-term harm to patients. Perhaps allopathy will soon find a better way to counter superbugs that grow more and more resilient. Ayurveda can possibly help in this regard. Only time will tell.

Perhaps the most crucial role of Ayurveda is in long-term restorative care, once the emergency has been dealt with.

Ayurveda Works Best for . . .

Ayurveda works best for diseases that are slow to progress, are multicausal and are related to lifestyle. This is how we could classify the fortes of Ayurveda:

- Chronic metabolic disorders or lifestyle diseases
- Skin diseases
- Arthritis and its types
- Degenerative diseases
- Management of post-stroke conditions
- Early diabetes
- Immunological diseases

Let's consider a case in point. A lady who was known to be diabetic came to us to get her leg treated. It had become gangrenous and the allopathic doctors she had previously consulted had suggested the removal of a toe. Quite mortified, she decided to try the Ayurvedic alternative. We began with a combination of massages and medicines to improve blood circulation around the affected area. After sometime, her toe bled during each massage, which was a clear sign that it was active. Six months later, she was back on her toes, literally.

The fact of the matter is that Ayurveda physicians, many times, are approached by patients only when allopathy fails. This is an extra burden to an Ayurveda physician.

Some more disturbing limitations:

1. Losing traditional wisdom to big pharma and MNC giants—for example, neem, turmeric and basmati.
2. Perhaps because of this, there is an unwillingness among certain Ayurveda practitioners to share their knowledge.

3. Very few incentives and recognition of local health practitioners and ancient healing traditions that have contributed to Ayurveda's understanding—by the medical community, or the governments.
4. Unwillingness among most practitioners to cognize and act in areas of natural resource availability, processing of herbs, etc.—areas that significantly affect the practice of Ayurveda.
5. Expensive quality-control measures that make it difficult for small-scale pharmacies to test their products.
6. Negative publicity and hurled criticisms quackery, pseudoscience—very few people ask questions to know—'What is it about?'; 'How can we validate it scientifically?'

Conclusion

Ayurveda has survived for as long as it has, thanks to the commitment of its loyal practitioners. But it is struggling for wider acceptance and support, and also to stay abreast of recent developments.

There is an increasing demand for local, accessible and affordable medical treatment—a need that Ayurveda can fulfil. Its potential can be fully tapped only when the limitations and regulations that hamper it are addressed from the ground up.

A revamped Ayurveda will be a boon to the world. Ayurveda's strengths align well with the emerging needs of society. We are suffering less from infections and more from our own actions. Like with changing a dysfunctional lifestyle, Ayurveda takes time and delivers long-term results.

Nobody said true restoration would be an easy promise to keep. But it's worth the wait and then some more.

10

The Summative Approach

Knowledge has no boundaries. When we humans began amassing large amounts of factual information about ourselves and the world, we felt the need to create specialized fields of knowledge. This allowed individuals to choose a field of knowledge and become experts in that. This worked well. No human can know everything. So we could create doctors who knew about the circulation of fluids in the human body and didn't have to concern themselves with the circulation of fluids inside an automobile.

Today, we are in the middle of a different kind of knowledge revolution. We know a lot more than we did when we began demarcating fields of knowledge. As a result, we are acutely aware of deep interconnections between various fields of knowledge. This has played out in two ways:

- **Experts of different fields together**: For instance, we have crafted our understanding of natural history by using many sciences such as archaeology, geology, botany, zoology, genealogy and, to some extent, anthropology.

- **New super-specialized fields get created**: For instance, astrophysics is an offshoot of astronomy, physics and chemistry. Even within astrophysics, deep areas of expertise have been created. Some study black holes, some others study the behaviour of stars, etc.

Can the same not happen for allopathy and Ayurveda? Can allopath doctors and Ayurveda doctors not work together? Also, can we look forward to generations of super-specialized doctors whose job will be to find intersection points between the two sciences?

Welcome to the exciting idea of summative medicine, where as always, the whole is greater than the sum of its parts.

YOUR medicine + MY medicine = MORE POWERFUL medicine
YOUR approach + MY approach = BETTER approach

And when it comes to allopathy and Ayurveda, the synergies are so strong that they jump out at you as soon as you begin a cursory exploration of the sciences.

The Best of Both Worlds

The Best of Allopathy	**The Best of Ayurveda**
Medicines and methodologies influenced by the latest research findings	Expertise developed over millennia
24x7 emergency healthcare	A patient and comprehensive approach
Modern diagnostic tools to quickly identify the disease	A willingness to go beyond disease management to deliver wellness

The table above hints at how the two sciences can unite in a marriage made in heaven.

Allopathy has the latest scientific breakthroughs—in the form of machines and medicines—at its disposal. When precious human life must be saved in seconds or even hours, the patient must turn to the allopath. Indeed, modern medicine works like a bullet. It has the power to kill the harmful pathogen instantaneously.

Ayurveda, on the other hand, works as an investigator. It takes time amassing clues and following the culprit pathogen's trail. But once the pathogen is cornered, it is banished forever. Ayurveda makes up for its slowness by being smart. It does not harm helpful microorganisms while doing its job, just like a good investigator protects blameless bystanders. Having said that, allopathy has helped Ayurveda become faster by offering modern diagnostic tools to the vaidya. Any worthwhile vaidya is adept at reading X-rays, CT/MRI scan results, ECG/EEG reports and, of course, any and every blood report. And when the vaidya is reading a report, he is interpreting it using wisdom distilled over millennia.

Thus, summative medicine is like a sharp investigator who is skilled in wielding firearms. Here, brain meets brawn and ancient knowledge meets modern science. Most importantly, the power of eliminating painful symptoms meets the magic of eliminating the root causes of the disease.

Many physicians on both sides of the divide want to dismiss the advantages offered by the other side. Some will be charitable enough to concede that the other side has advantages, but will quickly add that the two sciences are like railway tracks that must necessarily run parallel to each other without ever meeting.

However, the practitioner of summative medicine identifies various intersection points in the treatment process. S/he creates a methodology wherein the two systems can step in or step out as needed. The summative practitioner is able to bring a great deal of objectivity to the healing process—s/he refuses to be bound by the constraints of one science. For her/him, the needs of the patient are paramount.

Consider the simple example of a fifty-year-old patient with a blockage in an artery. Allopathy would typically use blood thinners and medicines to dilute the clot. This will help the patient stay active and functional but not offer any kind of comprehensive restoration. Here, Ayurveda can step in by prescribing lifestyle changes that will build resilience. It will also prescribe medicines that clear arterial blockages and prevent further accumulation of fat/calcium in the body.

In my experience, a whole host of diseases are best treated using a summative approach. These include anaemia, idiopathic thrombocytopenia, stroke, rheumatoid arthritis, liver disorders, osteoarthritis and skin diseases such as psoriasis.

Meanwhile, Ayurveda can offer better solutions in many diseases such as:

- Multicausal diseases—such as liver disorders and IBS
- Genetic disorders—such as autism
- Lifestyle diseases—such as diabetes

Given the synergies, it's perhaps easy to start believing that all is well with the union of Ayurveda and allopathy. We might eventually get there, but as of now, there are many problems to overcome.

Problem 1: The Summative Approach Doesn't Work for Many Diseases

In many diseases, a physician will exhibit recklessness by attempting a summative approach.

Disease	**Why the Summative Approach Fails**
Hypertension	An alpha or a beta blocker could be prescribed by the allopath to lower the blood pressure. Ayurveda will offer a medicine to work on the patient's *vyāna* vāyu. For BP to become normal, vyāna vāyu needs to function at its optimal level. If both medicines are taken at once, BP could drop really quickly and really low, putting the life of the patient at risk.
Diabetes	Allopathy medications help reduce blood sugar levels, while Ayurveda rejuvenates the functionality of beta cells. These two approaches don't work well together.

In both cases, one has to slowly withdraw one medicine, and gradually increase the other, together with lifestyle changes.

Of course, summative medicine is at its infancy and physicians from both sides might learn to combat these diseases together. For now, discretion is the better part of valour. No physician should attempt summative medicine without learning intensively about the pros and cons of the approach adopted by the physician from the other side.

Problem 2: Integration Is a Long Way Away

One day, true integration will happen. And all medical sciences will blend seamlessly with each other to offer the best care to the patient.

In an integrative model, the Ayurveda and allopathy physicians will proactively collaborate. They will understand each other, consult with each other and help build each other's knowledge base. For that to happen, these physicians have to overcome many barriers.

The Barrier of Language

If an Ayurveda physician says that tulsi (holy basil) is medicinal and can increase pitta, decrease aama and bring down jwara, the allopath may not understand. Instead, if the Ayurveda physician states that tulsi can aid homeostasis, the allopath will nod in understanding.

Concepts such as homeostasis of Claude Bernard and Walter Cannon, and the tridoṣas of Charaka and Sushruta, are based on common ideas and principles. Both talk about internal balance. I imagine a day when both terms are comfortably exchanged between the Ayurveda and allopathy physicians. On that day, an allopath will be able to read the profile and case history of a patient, as prepared by an Ayurvedic physician, without blinking an eyelid.

Today, without a shared vocabulary, integration remains a pipe dream. Ayurveda needs to translate the language it has been using for centuries into the more commonly understood language of modern science. Meanwhile, the allopath can explore the seemingly exotic terms used in Ayurveda.

The Barrier of Methodology

The average time that an Ayurveda physician spends with a patient is many times higher than that of an allopath. During the patient's first visit, their prakṛti needs to be determined, and this can take time. Also, the Ayurveda physician is constantly on the lookout for mental or emotional triggers to a physical ailment. An allopath specializing in integrative medicine might also have to invest more time. This might increase the cost for the patient or reduce the income of the allopath. Alternatively, efficiencies will have to be built into the methodology so that the allopath can spend the same amount of time to absorb more information coming from Ayurvedic diagnoses.

The Barrier of Pharmacology

Ayurveda arrives at the patient's bedside with an exhaustive list of medicines extracted from nature. An allopath needs to double his/her knowledge of medicines to integrate with Ayurveda. S/he needs to understand not only the use of plants by human beings, but also the nature, qualities and effects of each medicine. This is called the tattva (principle) stage of study—the third and ultimate stage of understanding, as per Ayurveda.

The first stage of understanding is *vyavahara* (business/operation), where the physician acquires a basic understanding of the concepts. This is followed by the shastra (technique) stage, where the reasoning behind the concepts is understood.

To reach the tattva stage of understanding, the allopath will have to put in as much effort as the Ayurveda physician did while doing the undergraduate course. That requires commitment. So one can imagine such an allopath pursuing integrative medicine as a specialized master's programme. For this to happen, universities will have to offer well-designed master's programmes. It's going to be a long journey.

The Barrier of Administering Medicines

Although Ayurveda uses some modern technologies while processing plant extracts, it is riddled with an inherent problem of bulk reduction. Raw materials for Ayurveda medicines are typically used in large quantities and condensing them is difficult. The minimum amount of kaṣāya (decoction) administered is about 50–60 ml. Meanwhile, other medicines have to be mixed with water, etc.

Can these medicines be administered using a capsule, tablet or a syringe? Can some of them be pumped into an IV drip without distorting their essence? These questions can only be answered when technologies and processes integrate more effectively.

Moreover, administering these medicines will require added infrastructure and staff training.

Needless to say, the Ayurveda physician will also have to put in the same amount of effort into exploring modern medicine.

Given the gap between the ideal future and today, I have used the word 'summative' and not 'integrative' in the title of this chapter. In the summative approach, the Ayurveda and allopathic physicians are aware of each other's presence while offering care to the same patient, but do not collaborate.

However, as the head of a clinic that offers summative cures, I know that the summative approach is already superior to the care administered by Ayurveda or allopathy alone. Let me demonstrate this using a case study.

Case Study: Back to Mobility

History

A sixty-four-year-old man, a known hypertensive person who suffered a stroke a month ago, was struggling with minimal movement in his right hand, difficulty walking, incontinence of bladder, impaired speech and depression.

He had a history of falling. In this instance, even though he gained consciousness immediately after his fall, he had problems moving his right hand and leg, and had slurred speech. He was rushed to an allopathic hospital, where he was diagnosed with hemiplegia because of multiple clots in the brain and blocked carotid arteries (50 per cent), which led to the paralysis of the right side of his body. He was depressed because of his helpless condition.

He was prescribed blood thinners, anti-hypertensive medicines, multivitamins and other oral medicines by the neuroscience department. Though he was advised a diagnostic angiogram, his caregivers thought that he would be able to recover through Ayurveda therapies. Thus, he was brought to me.

Personal Pathophysiological Profile

The initial personal profiling revealed:

Factor	**Focal Points**	**Impact on Treatment**
Dūṣya, doṣa and dhātu (functional and structural tissues)	Kapha and vāta doṣa impairment; rasa, rakta, māṁsa, medās were impacted	Multiple dhātu and doṣa were involved and hence multi-model treatments had to be planned

Bhoomi deśa (location)	Anūpa deśa (marshy)	Kapha doṣa aggravation was possible
Rogi bala (strength)	Madhyama (medium)	Only moderate potency medicine can be given in medium dosage
Kāla (season)	Spring	Kapha accumulation would lead to obstruction of channels in the body. Hence kapha doṣa mitigating treatments had to be planned in the beginning
Anala (digestive fire)	Low	Improper digestion led to a lack of nourishment of other dhātu
Prakṛti (constitution)	Kapha–vāta	Treatment was planned such that praakrutha doṣa was not affected
Vaya (age)	Middle age	Multi-model treatments could be planned along with virechana and basti treatments
Satva (mental strength)	Medium	Owing to the madhayma satva, decent tolerance and cooperation could be expected during the treatment
Sātmya (way of life)	Moderate physical activities	Not relevant in the case of a fall victim's treatment
Āhāra (food)	Non-vegetarian south Indian food	Vegetarian food was advised

Treatment

We took the allopathic diagnosis as the first step and enhanced the case history by Ayurvedic pathophysiological profiling of the patient, as detailed above. This allowed us to offer customized treatment focusing on the kapha and vāta doṣa impairments.

Over the course of twenty-five days, diverse topical and systemic treatments were implemented. These included dhanyamladhara, virechana, talapodichil, ksheeradhooma, nasya, sarvangaabhyanga, patrapindasweda, shiropichu, pizhichil, marma massage, yoga basti, shastika shali pinda sweda, jihwa lepa and pichu on painful joints, along with monitored suitable oral medications. As an integrative approach, he was also advised physiotherapy and speech therapy.

The cumulative result of the therapies was as follows:

- The initial sroto shodhana removed blockages of the srotas of the body to expel toxins as virechana helped to cleanse the GI tract and enhanced the medicine absorption.
- The basti may have helped in balancing the vāta doṣa.
- Various kinds of sarvanga treatments helped in relieving stiffness and swelling by stimulating and providing deep nourishment and rejuvenating of dhātu of the body.
- These treatments also helped in reducing stress and inducing good sleep.

Name of the Treatment	**Description of the Treatment**	**Impact on the Body**
Pañca karma treatments were administered as described below		
Dhanyamladhara	Warm fermented medicated water poured on the body	Helps in combating the kapha and vāta doṣas, releasing stiffness of joints
Ksheeradhooma	Medicated milk fomentation	Helps in reducing facial muscle stiffness, with vasodilatation action, and also helps in stimulating the nerves connected to the facial muscles

Shiropichu	Warm oil pack applied on the vertex	Balances the impaired vāta, nourishes the nervous system; reduces intracranial oedema and dilutes clots, if any
Talapodichil	Herbal paste applied on the head	Stimulates the nerves; provides nootropic effect
Patrapindasweda	A special type of fomentation with fresh herbal leaves	Helps in improving blood circulation to the affected part and relieving pain and stiffness of the muscles and joints; improves the muscular tone through its *vātahara* property
Nasya	Medicated oil drops administered through the nose	Helps in cleansing the *srotas* (microchannel) of the head; helps the medicines reach the brain quickly
Virechana	Therapeutic purgation	Helps in expelling the toxins from the body; thus helps the body to absorb the medications more effectively
Sarvangaabhyanga	Full body massage	Improves the circulation of the whole body; relieves muscle stiffness, strengthens the ligaments, tendons, joints; and also induces good sleep, which reduces stress and relaxes the mind; balances all the doṣas, especially vāta
Pizhichil	Warm medicated oil poured on the whole body using a special method for seven days (one hour each)	Helps deep nourishment and lubrication of all the dhātus of the body and thereby rejuvenates them; stimulates the neuromuscular systems

Marma massage	Special type of massage on vital points of the body	Enhances the blood supply to the dhātus and tones the tendons and muscles, helps in restoring the vāta
Yoga basti	Cleansing and nourishing enemas	Helps in detoxification and especially balancing the vāta; also helps in lubricating, and nourishing the dhātus
Shastikashalipinda sweda	Special treatment with medicated milk and rice bolus fomentation for seven days (one hour each)	Helps in fortifying the dhātus and recovering the muscle tone
Jihwalepa	Herbal application on tongue	Helps in toning of the sublingual muscles and thus promotes salivation, enhances the taste perception, and also might help in improving speech
Pichu	Warm oil packs	Strengthens ligaments and tendons of the joints; relieves stiffness
Physiotherapy	Physiotherapy	Helps in bringing in muscular mobility and makes the body active
Speech therapy	Speech therapy	Helps in tongue movement through therapeutic guidance

After twenty-five days of this integrative approach, he was given reviews by neurosurgeons regarding his allopathy medications, and also advised physiotherapy and speech therapy.

At the time of discharge, the patient was able to walk confidently and independently for short durations and his speech had improved noticeably. Bowel movement was brought to normalcy and bladder control was regained.

He was an outpatient for two more months and he recovered well. His family members were thrilled to see him function independently. Contrary to their expectations, he could converse with them again.

Conclusion

Knowledge has no ego. It doesn't and shouldn't matter where a great idea came from. This is doubly important when human lives are at stake. Both allopathy and Ayurveda are replete with great concepts and both can work together magically to offer the best care possible to the patient.

Since the sciences are synergistically aligned, thought leaders on both sides need to inch closer together. Let them retain their scepticism while they do so. But let them lose their cynicism.

Meanwhile, the government of India has taken a bold step by creating the Ministry of AYUSH—which stands for Ayurveda, Yoga, Naturopathy, Unani, Siddha and Homoeopathy. Perhaps this ministry should be renamed 'AYUSHA'—with one of the As meaning Allopathy.

The efficient allopathy must marry the restorative Ayurveda. The two have been engaged for a long time already. Practitioners of summative medicine will tell you that the courtship has been joyous. With more people joining the bandwagon, we might soon hear the wedding bells ring loud and clear across the globe.

11

The Future

In a small village in Tamil Nadu, people stand in queues to buy oil previously used in electrical transformers. Turns out that the electrical transformers installed in every nook and corner of the country use a particular type of mineral oil for insulation, as a coolant and for other requirements. At some point in time, maybe serendipitously or maybe because of a lack of resources, somebody discovered that this oil was very effective in treating joint pain caused by rheumatoid arthritis.

This example reflects the ethos of an entire civilization. Indians are known to use scarcity as motivation to find quaint solutions. In fact, the science of Ayurveda has itself been built on such innovations and discoveries—painstakingly accumulated over a long period of time.

Ayurveda welcomes such discoveries into its purview and finds a way to incorporate them. A good Ayurveda acharya will observe any given phenomenon, study it, understand its impact and use it in healthcare practices.

This is why I argue that Ayurveda is an adaptable, thriving, growing science. Ayurveda was, is and will always be owned by the people who use it—enriching their lives and being enriched by them. It would be a shame if this science is diminished because of the limitations it currently experiences.

So, as we approach the end of this book, I would like to point out the major areas in which we need solutions. I will also be bold enough to suggest somc of those solutions. For these solutions to come into play, many stakeholders—such as Ayurveda practitioners, agriculturists, botanists, chemists and other experts—need to work with government agencies. They need to influence policies as well as implement important initiatives.

Here are the broad areas where solutions must be found.

Cultivation of Plants

Today, if 20 per cent of Indians using allopathic medicines shift to Ayurveda, many of our medicinal plants will reach the brink of extinction.

Cultivation is not the first choice for plants used by Ayurveda. The medicinal properties of Ayurveda plants can be attributed to their secondary metabolites. A majority of these secondary metabolites are acquired in the wild from the surrounding plants and environment. Medicinal plants grown in a farm as a monoculture lack this exposure. Additionally, an abundance of artificial water supply, fertilizers and other resources make the plant weak. So farms tend to create large yields of impotent medicinal plants.

- Turmeric from drylands such as Tamil Nadu, Rajasthan and the hilly areas of the North-East is known to have a high level of curcumin, which increases its potency. The curcumin level in farm-grown turmeric is significantly lower and therefore not useful for medicinal purposes.
- Similarly, ashwagandha (Rennet/*Withania somnifera*), which grows naturally in Rajasthan and the Kutch area of Gujarat, makes excellent medicine. However, attempts to grow ashwagandha in the Coimbatore area of Tamil Nadu and the Palakkad area of Kerala have failed miserably due to excessive watering. The plant's roots became starchy and almost bereft of medicinal properties. New research has helped farmers in Tamil Nadu grow ashwagandha in the appropriate soil and in the right climatic and irrigation conditions.
- It is well known that sandalwood is a root parasite that cannot be grown in isolation. It is necessary to have supportive trees around it for effective yield.
- We need such research for other plants and trees required by Ayurveda, including amla (Indian gooseberry), reetha (*Sapindus mukorossi*), shekakai (*Acacia concinna*), drumsticks (*Moringa oleifera*), aloe vera, isabgol (*Psyllium*), senna (*Cassia angustifolia*), poppy seeds, sarpagandha, ashwagandha, bel (*Aegle marmelos*), bringaraj (False daisy/*Eclipta prostrate*), musali (*Chlorophytum borivilianum*), jatropha (nettlespurge), tulsi (holy basil) and jamun (*Syzygium cumini*), the five trees that make up the famous Dashamoolas (the other five being herbs).

Guggulu: Endangered Species and Cultivation

Guggulu (Indian bdellium-tree/*Commiphora wightii*) is a medicinal plant grown in Rajasthan and Gujarat. It is used to make medicines that treat obesity and rheumatoid arthritis. It has been listed as critically endangered by the World Conservation Union. It takes about five to seven years for it to be ready for harvest. As the demand increased, the cutting of these shrubs also increased. This unsustainable practice led to its endangerment.

A friend of mine, a senior botanist, told me that he had developed a sustainable method to harvest the gum. He had strived to propagate this method. The challenge: the set ways of collectors who have been cutting down the shrub for years.

In the recent past, however, farmers started cultivating guggulu and adopted my friend's healthy and sustainable way of harvesting gum. A movement began in Rajasthan and Gujarat to save this plant. Since then, land has been allotted for the cultivation of the plant and only sustainable harvesting methods are being used. This, and other such projects, show the way to a better future.

I repeat: Most Ayurveda plants should not be grown as monoculture. While the need for farm-based cultivation might be inevitable, it is imperative that such farms replicate the biodiversity of the wild. Here are the factors that we need to study in detail for each plant:

- The habitat—which includes the altitude, climatic conditions and the microbiome and microbiology of the surrounding plants.
- The impact of the use of fertilizers, irrigation and other farming techniques.
- The cultivation methodology—including the manner in which the target plant will be grown alongside other plants that offer secondary metabolites.

It is imperative to undertake this research at breakneck speed, considering the increasing demand and depleting natural resources that may threaten the sustainability of Ayurveda. The good news is that the research need not start from scratch. Botany and *Vruksh* Ayurveda have identified useful plants, understood their chemical compositions, their habitats, growth promoters, micro-environment and other aspects. We have to find a way to integrate these two sciences and propagate their findings.

The government has a crucial role to play in fomenting such collaborations. It can also do things that individual farmers cannot.

Unlike an individual farmer, the government has the land and patience to wait for ten to fifteen years—which is the time it takes for some of Ayurveda's plants to yield a harvest. Take, for example, the ten roots that go into the making of *dashamoolarișța*. Some of these roots can be harvested only after ten to fifteen years. The government can explore the use of wastelands to cultivate such medicinal plants. This will include lands adjacent to railway track and highways—along with land deemed unsuitable for conventional agriculture.

This is a much better idea than planting non-indigenous species, such as eucalyptus, whose primary allure is that they grow fast.

As an added benefit, when one plants medicinal herbs and trees, one encourages its exposure to the general public and fosters research in required cultivation methodologies.

Now let's take a broader look at how the government can lead us into the twenty-first century, in which Ayurveda can reclaim its glory.

Government Initiatives and Policies

The Union Government of India has acknowledged Ayurveda to be on a par with allopathic medicine. This is most evident in the formation of the Ministry of AYUSH in 2014. Due to this and other reasons, insurance companies have started covering Ayurveda treatments. These are welcome changes.

However, one cannot help but notice that every time, the entire budget for the Ministry of AYUSH is the same as the budget allocation for one allopathic institution—AIIMS in New Delhi. In the 2021 Budget, the AYUSH Ministry got a mere Rs 2,970 crore, which is only 4.2 per cent of the health budget (Rs 71,269 crore). It's safe to say that the Union government's heart is opening up to Ayurveda, but its purse strings are sewn tight. Whereas the state government in Kerala recently announced Rs 3 billion and 300 acres of land for the establishment of the International Research Institute of Ayurveda.

There is a need for such investments. Perhaps it will also be a good idea to nominate one of the existing institutes—or a totally new one—as the apex body of the science. This institute will work closely with the AYUSH Ministry and be the de facto leader of the science of Ayurveda in India. It will champion worthwhile initiatives in the spheres of research, education, agriculture, entrepreneurship and pharmaceuticals. This apex body will act as the conduit between the government and the rest of society.

Also, through this apex body or the Ministry of AYUSH directly, the government needs to formulate comprehensive policy changes in multiple realms, starting with education.

Education

Centralized Syllabus

Today, all over India, Bachelor of Ayurveda, Medicine, and Surgery (BAMS) students study the same syllabus. While this sounds great, there is an issue that needs to be addressed.

A standardized syllabus means that students from the length and breadth of the country get no exposure to local botany and local healing techniques. So students practising in a desert region might have received minimal exposure to the ailments afflicting their patients. This is akin to a Siberian doctor not receiving training to treat hypothermia or a student in the equatorial jungles receiving only one session in the treatment of malaria.

It makes sense for students to study the unique plants available locally and the unique treatments that people of the region have successfully practised for ages. While the basic course needs to be standardized, individual educational institutions should be allowed to customize the course to impart locally relevant knowledge.

Another point to be considered: The human anatomy is studied using the approach followed by Western medicine. Perhaps some curriculum time can be allocated to understanding the unique anatomical perspectives brought forth by Ayurveda.

The post-independent India's political scenario is dominated by a Western model, especially in the areas of education, development and health. Contrary to the Gandhian philosophy of Swaraj and his critiques on modern Western civilization, the political leadership in India has ignored the views of thinkers such as Gandhiji.

While the Nehruvian idea of development has helped us achieve success in certain areas, it has done damage to indigenous knowledge systems and indigenous notions of development.

Keeping this scenario in the backdrop, one should look into the development of institutionalized education of Ayurveda in India.

By an Act of Parliament in 1975, the Central Council for Indian Medicine (CCIM) came into existence to regularize and bring uniform standards into the Ayurvedic education in the country. Thus, the basic reason for establishing CCIM as a national body was itself based on a distorted understanding of Ayurveda as a conventional system of medicine like modern biomedicine, which is comfortable with a uniform syllabus.

Curriculum & Syllabus

Is a uniform syllabus for Ayurveda desirable?

The strength and beauty of Ayurveda lies in its diversity. Ayurveda has been enriched with contributions from various scholars, different ethnic cultures and floristic diversity over a long period of time.

Each geographical area in India has come up with various applications of Ayurvedic practice. For example, Kerala has a rich tradition based on Sahasrayoga, Chikitsamanjari, Yogamrutham, Arogyakalpadrumam and experiences of Ashta Vaidya traditions.

Likewise, Karnataka has various texts and procedures in Ayurvedic treatment based on the region's experience, climate and flora.

Maharashtra is rich in practices based on regional classics. For instance, the state has traditional places of excellence such as Nanal traditions similar to the Ashta Vaidya tradition of Kerala.

The state of Kashmir has a Kashmiri version parallel to *Charaka Samhita*, which has recently been re-edited by interested groups.

Rajasthan and Uttar Pradesh are well known for their use of minerals, metals and other rare plants of that area. The use of oils, ghritams and kwathas are not very popular in their practice.

We do not see any of this regional excellence reflected in the syllabus. The student who comes out of the current uniform curriculum is kept away from his or her own regional excellence in a given area. If a student comes out of a Kerala college and is not exposed to the centres of Ayurveda practice prevalent in Kerala itself but outside the university, he or she will not be able to understand or assimilate the Kerala special treatments such as *Dhara*, *Pizichil*, *Kizhi* and *Kadivasthi*.

A more balanced way of framing a syllabus for Ayurveda should have taken into consideration this regional excellence. Thus the uniformity of the syllabus poses a great danger of extinction to all the regional diversity in Ayurveda, unless we act consciously to bring those elements back into the curriculum.

Another serious concern for Ayurveda practitioners is the structure of the syllabus. The structure is, unfortunately, a distorted replica of the modern medicine curriculum. It should be known that Ayurveda has its own pedagogy, which has laid down certain principles and methods for teaching Ayurveda.

Slokas, chapters and sthanas are all interconnected. We must teach Ayurveda through the traditional, classical approach, reflected in the way the Samhitas are written, rather than disintegrating it into subjects that mimic the syllabi of biomedicine. The traditional textbook-based learning helps the student to understand the overall perspective of the science.

If one seriously goes through the chapters of a classical text, from *Suthrasthana* to *Uttarasthana* of Vagbhata, one can perceive the rhythm and the ambience of the shastra. *Ashtanga Hrudayam* is a typical example of how a healing science can be put into a precise and logical form with minimum words. On the contrary, if you divide Ayurveda into modern subject categories, the holistic approach of the knowledge system is lost and the student will not be able to use the *thantra yukthis* (the logical methods for understanding and interpreting the medical texts) to dissect and elaborate on the implicit meanings of words. The student can thus have only superficial comprehension of the subject.

The Story of *Charaka Samhita*

Interestingly, the syllabus for graduates has the *Charaka Samhita* as two papers: 'Charakam Poorvardham' and 'Charakam Uttarardham'. *Charaka Samhita* was originally edited by sequencing the contents from *Suthrasthana* to *Sidhisthana,* covering all its topics in a methodical and logical way. The original text has neither *Poorvardham* nor *Uttarardham.*

Some publisher in Varanasi could not bind the book as a single volume, and so, for easy handling, he made it into *Poorvardham* (first half) and *Uttarardham* (last half). Ironically our curriculum simply adopted this *Poorvardham* as one paper and *Uttarardham* as another paper for learning and examination.

This has no logic and offers no explanation as to how a graduate-level student can understand *Charaka Samhita*—a whole multidisciplinary subject—as a non-detailed textbook (as we do in a literature course).

Language

If one has to learn Siddha, knowledge of Tamil is essential. If one needs to study Unani, knowledge of Urdu is a must. If one has to learn modern medicine, knowledge of English is a prerequisite. Ayurveda, however, can be learnt in any Indian language, although Sanskrit is the key to Ayurvedic literature.

In India, generally all Sanskrit-based technical knowledge is safeguarded from unscrupulous hands and made more rigorous by optimally using the grammar, rhythm, metre and other literary talents. A word, by its contextual significance, can have different meanings and can change its connotations or technical implicit meaning. For example, the word '*saindhava*' in a dining context means a particular type of salt and, in the context of a battlefield, means 'horse'.

All these aspects are lost while learning the original texts through a translation. The classics in Ayurveda are better explained by earlier commentators such as Je Jjada, Chakradatta, Dhrudabala, Aruna Datta, Hemadri, etc., who are very adept at the intricacies of the Sanskrit language and the Ayurvedic practice. Once the mere translations are fed to the students without the original understanding of the text, the students do not understand the complexity of the materials and thus are not inspired to go deeper into the shastra.

As a result, even a sincere academic institution can churn out, at best, only a good technical-level physician, not a research-minded scientist, who can make original contributions to the science, as was happening until the seventeenth century, when the last authoritative book on Ayurveda came to light.

Entrance

Most of the students who join Ayurveda are non-selected candidates of MBBS. For them, this is just a profession in some way connected to modern medicine, and since there is no other way to get into the practice of medicine, they have taken Ayurveda as an excuse to practise allopathy. Thus, at the entry level itself, Ayurveda is getting a mismatched candidate who has no mind to learn or practise Ayurveda. To add fuel to the situation, there is no inspiring introduction given to the student, so that the non-enthusiast is converted to a well-informed student of Ayurveda.

Teaching

The foundational principles of Ayurveda are based on the *Darsanik* worldview, which is the basis of understanding Ayurveda from its roots. A student who is initiated into this science needs to develop a close acquaintance with the premises of Ayurveda. Traditionally, Ayurveda was taught to the students after *kavya* (literature), *vyakarana* (grammar) and *tharka* (logic). It is said that to become a student of Ayurveda, a working knowledge of the above three aspects are necessary. A student coming out of twelve years of grooming under modern education cannot understand the Ayurvedic philosophy unless the student is given enough time for acquainting himself/herself with the basic pillars of Ayurveda.

This can be achieved if one or two academic years are devoted to tharka, vyakarana and kavya.

There was a scheme in CCIM in the 1970 to have a seven-and-a-half-year BAMS course for students who have passed the Class X, wherein the initial two years were dedicated exclusively to the above three components and biology, chemistry and physics, which is equivalent to Class XII. This model would have been better due to three reasons:

(1) For a seven-and-a-half-year-long professional course, only those who are really interested in the subject will come. As this decision of joining Ayurveda has to be taken at the time of completing Class X, the entrance exam drop-outs of other systems will not come to study Ayurveda.
(2) In case one feels that one cannot fit into the system, he/she can quit after finishing the pre-medical (two years) and opt for any other science graduation without losing any years of study.
(3) The student gets sufficient time to integrate with Ayurvedic philosophy in a span of two years. By the time he/she gets into the main Ayurvedic course, he/she will be intellectually prepared to assimilate a new thinking process based on Ayurvedic principles. This is the most crucial part of Ayurvedic education.

Method

Education in an Indian context is a complete transformation of the personality from teacher to the taught.

Ideally, the main subjects, such as Suthra, Nidana, Chikitsa and Utthara, should be taught by a single experienced teacher and he/she should be the person to take the student from the first year until the internship is over. The interpretations and applications of theories in Ayurveda and the core subjects should be taken by this senior teaching faculty. In a five-year course, there should, therefore, be five gurus leading a team with him or her as a main thread for the whole of five years.

This does not mean that we should abolish all the present departmental facilities.

There is ample scope for reorganizing the curriculum and faculty in an aptly arranged way, which will allow free flow of information. The supportive departments (non-core subjects) such as Dravyaguna, Rasasastras, Visha, Kalpa and other special branches, can be separately taught by different teachers.

The pre-clinical and clinical division of the medicine is also unnecessary. The vaidyas used to take the students to the patient from the very first day onwards—not to involve them in the treatment but to introduce them to the different aspects of treatment.

Recent medical education reformation in certain states in the USA has also taken this path of introducing students to the clinical environment the first year onwards.

Pedagogy

Indian traditional pedagogy introduced a unique mode of learning process based on the following four steps—Adheethi, Bodha, Acharana and Pracharana.

(a) *Adheethi:* It is the first-hand learning of the subject. Therefore it is like feeding data into hardware. We feed certain codified information to our memory without actually going into its detailed interpretation. This is more relevant when the information is given in a metered form of lyrics, as it is easy to remember this.

One will be able to recollect it in its full form at any time and will be able to analyse it before use in a given context. This is especially important in *Dravyagunam* and formulation indications.

(b) *Bodha:* It is the second stage of learning, wherein the student is empowered by the teacher to analyse the meaning of the verses with *poorvapara sambandha* (with reference to the previous and forthcoming aspects).

For example, when one learns the verse 'Ragadi Rogan' (the first sloka of *Ashtanga Hrudayam*), the bodha component of learning takes the students to the concept of *manas* (mind), its aberration (raga), states such as kama, *krodha, moha and mada-matsarya,* and association of these states with the origin of physical diseases.

The teacher, if enlightened, may be able to explain why the acharya used the mental aberration 'raga' at the start of a classical text on medicine, ignoring more important diseases such as jwara, which is the basis of all diseases.

The teacher may further split the word 'raga' into 'ra' and 'ga', which as per numerology, means 'two' (ra) and 'three' (ga), respectively. This indicates the importance of *manodosha*s rajas and tamas, and also of vata, pitta and kapha as *sariradosha*s (physical factors) in disease origin.

Thus the first two lines of the sloka of Vagbhata can be explained (bodha) to show their interconnections.

(c) *Acharana:* This is self-practice. The acharya says that even if God Himself comes and says that the sun rises in the west, one should not accept it because one can see that it is not the case.

Whatever *aptavachanas* (authoritative words) are there should be put into the crucible of self-experimentation. This can be your own clinical practice or objective studies of any kind.

(d) *Pracharana:* This is preaching or teaching. In the last stage of learning, one becomes an integral part of the knowledge itself and will have no doubt of its application or presentation. Only at this stage is one allowed to teach or train others in the given subject.

These four steps very briefly explained here give an ideal picture of the learning process in India as practised by our intellectuals of yore.

Why is it that we cannot adopt these methods in present-day teaching? This can be achieved without disturbing the present infrastructure and facilities of teaching. The only things needed are reorientation and review of the situation.

Tattva, Shastra & Vyavahara

Tattva (the principle), shastra (the treatise) and vyavahara (the practice) are the three aspects of a knowledge system.

Tattva: The radical understanding of the fundamental principles of a science is tattva. Normally, the tattva level can be achieved by *aptas* who go beyond all the mental aberrations, can have enlightenment through self-realization and can experience the phenomenal truth without the help of any *upadhi* (tools).

The Indian science is supposed to have been written by people who have the tattva level of understanding. They are the rishis at the level of Atreya, Punarvasu, Charaka, Sushrut and Vagbhata.

Shastra: This is understanding the basis of the science from its paradigm and interpreting these universal principles to relate to applications. The concepts of pañca mahābhūtas, the origin of the universe and evolutionary stages, prakṛti and purusha, and recodification of pañca mahābhūtas into tridoṣas in the body as functional units, are the masterly craftsmanship of the *Sastrakaras.*

Vyavahara: A science based on universal principles such as heat and cold and five basic elements, which, when applied to local situations, has tremendous adaptation possibilities. This diversity in its application to different geographical areas and ethnic communities is the beauty of Ayurveda.

This strength of Ayurveda is not imbibed into the educational system, so the use of bio-resources as medicine becomes stagnant and sacrosanct. One does not understand that these classical formulations are only an example of the possibilities and not exhaustive. Even though the acharya says this explicitly ('*Ethat Budhimatam Udaharanamatram*'), we do not apply it.

An Experience

This model of education based on the classical method was partially implemented successfully in Coimbatore for ten years (1978–1988) by the AVR Foundation. The result was so encouraging that all the ten batches that came out of this institute either were hand-picked by the society or themselves became institutions. They are now spreading the true message of Ayurveda worldwide.

Ayurveda Nursing Education

Till date, Ayurveda has been using nurses who have been trained to serve patients seeking allopathic care. But if an acharya has nurses trained in Ayurveda, he/she would be able to treat more patients. Thankfully, there is an increase in the number of institutions offering courses in Ayurveda nursing. The government needs to incentivize this move in the right direction.

Harvesting and Research

The process of harvesting medicinal plants from natural sources is most often unsustainable. Do plants have to be uprooted or cut for us to benefit from them? Similarly, should animals be killed for us to extract medicinal components from them?

We urgently need government mandates to make all forms of harvesting sustainable and humane. These mandates can draw data from ongoing research in the area.

For instance, we may invent new biotechnological methods to replicate precious resources. How wonderful would it be if we are able to create musk in a laboratory? Can a DNA attached to a bacteria secrete musk just like we are able to do with insulin? By this, I mean the creation of musk as it is available naturally and not as a synthesized molecule. We would not only be able to prevent the inordinate slaying of musk deer, we would also be able to propagate the medicinal properties of musk. We need such research projects to bring modern perspectives to harvesting.

International Collaborations

The government will do well to sign MoUs with overseas governments and institutions so that key knowledge is shared and developed in unison. We discuss this further in the 'Ayurveda Worldwide' section below.

Pharmaceutical Regulations

Rigorous policies and standards exist to ascertain the quality and efficacy of medicines manufactured by allopathic pharmaceuticals. We need such regulations for Ayurvedic medicines too. This is such a basic need that its absence is shocking.

Today, Ayurveda physicians use trial-and-error methods to figure out the efficacy of medicines available in the market. Even then, there is no sure-fire way to know that these bottled medicines contain all the components in the required proportions. What if, due to the unavailability of some bark or root, it has not been added as an ingredient? We do not have a desirable answer to this and other such questions.

Therefore, regulations should take the form of:

1. **Establishing standards:** With policies that will unambiguously tell pharmaceutical companies what is expected of them. Standards will include the manner in which raw materials are to be collected, processed and packaged.
2. **Implementing standards:** We need an agency that will monitor all Ayurveda pharmaceutical companies and ensure that standards are met. This agency will have broad powers to impose punitive actions on erring companies.

3. **Ascertaining standards:** We need laboratories that will measure the quality of medicines manufactured by the companies. These laboratories will be able to determine the presence and proportions of all ingredients mentioned on the label. While it is easier to do so when one synthesizes molecules as allopathy does, nevertheless we must find a way to do so.

Integration with Chemistry

While chemistry has been used in Ayurveda to understand dosages better and to improve extraction methods, we haven't had an authentic collaboration between Ayurveda and chemistry. Even those pharmaceutical companies that manufacture only Ayurveda medicines seem to prefer synthesizing useful molecules rather than holistically manufacturing medicines. This is partly due to the absence of dialogue between experts in chemistry and experts in Ayurveda.

Ayurveda needs the help of chemists to determine the intrinsic nature of herbs, including the role played by primary and secondary metabolites. Additionally, they can tell us how to process and proportion each plant/herb with other substances.

Standards emerging from this collaboration can guide the formulation of pharmaceutical regulations described above.

Utilizing Manuscripts

An initiative titled Saving India's Medical Manuscripts identified over 1,00,000 medicinal manuscripts spread across the country as worthy of retaining for posterity. These are available in various libraries, prominent among which is the Saraswati Mahal library in Tanjore.

Meanwhile, the initiative also established that some important manuscripts have already left India and are now to be found in the Wellcome Collection in London and many institutes in Germany, the USA, the Netherlands and EU countries.

This treasure trove of knowledge needs to be brought back into circulation. Research scholars need to be funded so that they can collate these manuscripts, understand them, translate them and tell the rest of the world how we can use this knowledge to address today's global health problems.

Incidentally, I have edited a book, *Saving India's Medical Manuscripts*, published by the National Manuscript Mission, New Delhi, Government of India, and is available on Amazon.

Ongoing Research Findings

For long, Ayurveda has been considered an exotic field originating from a mysterious land. Finally, the West is willing to study it, not as an inexplicable phenomenon, but a science that deserves to be understood.

As a result, research projects are being conducted across the world.

- Research conducted by the National Health Interview Survey* in the USA talks about alternative therapies used by people with musculoskeletal pain. Massage therapy, yoga, meditation, hypnosis, Ayurveda, acupuncture, homoeopathy and naturopathy are shown to effect improvements in the quality of life led by patients.

---

* Deborah Brauser, 'Alternative Pain Management Common Among Patients With Musculoskeletal Pain', *Medscape*, 14 October 2016, http://www.medscape.com/viewarticle/870292

- Studies* have shown that alternative forms of medicine, including Ayurveda, have effectively addressed premature ejaculation. This can lead to the safer treatment of this ailment.
- Research shows that almost half the people suffering from dermatology issues have used complementary and alternative medicine (CAM). Some of the medicines used in Ayurveda, particularly curcumin and neem bark, have been proven effective in curing skin diseases.

As Ayurveda begins to produce more evidence acceptable to the modern scientific framework, more such research projects are bound to be undertaken. A reinforcing cycle of trust and transparency can thus be created.

Ayurveda Worldwide

A Viable Alternative

Germany, France, Hungary, Switzerland, Italy, Russia, Qatar and the USA are some of the countries that have shown immense interest in the science of Ayurveda.

- The European Ayurveda Association points out the initiatives taken by the European Union to study and promote Ayurveda. Its list of objectives includes coverage of Ayurveda treatments under insurance, encouraging the patient's choice of therapy, enabling authentic Ayurveda practices and implementing safety standards in Ayurvedic products.

---

* Katy Cooper et al, 'Complementary and Alternative Medicine for Management of Premature Ejaculation: A Systematic Review', *Sexual Medicine*, 30 December 2016, http://www.smoa.jsexmed.org/article/S2050-1161(16)30072-1/fulltext

- In the UK, where an overburdened NHS is finding it difficult to provide fast, reliable and quality healthcare, Ayurveda is mooted as a viable alternative. Ayurveda's ability to prevent diseases and promote health is making many in the UK sit up and take notice.
- In Qatar, Ayurveda practitioners are encouraged to register their practice and offer healthcare.
- In Russia, Ayurveda has managed to create a space for itself. Universities and educational institutions are undertaking research projects to understand and embrace Ayurveda.
- In the USA, even though the practice of Ayurveda as an alternative to allopathic medicine is not legal, it can be implemented as part of CAM (complementary and alternative medicine). Ayurveda practitioners can offer massage services and suggestions on diet and nutrition supplements. It is also possible to purchase Ayurveda medicines online even if FDA approvals are pending.

What might really get the engine roaring is a summative or integrative approach, as described in the chapter titled 'The Summative Approach'. But we need to successfully and widely implement the summative approach in India before we can expect the world to follow suit.

Collaborative Opportunities

Ayurveda and Traditional Chinese Medicine (TCM) have influenced each other in the past. Anecdotal accounts and circumstantial evidence make the following claims:

- Buddhist monks who travelled back and forth between India and China helped spread these practices in both countries.

- Some TCM techniques of anaesthesia and ophthalmology originated in India.
- Many Ayurveda texts were translated into Chinese languages.
- Indian Ayurvedic doctors were allowed to practice in China
- Some plants used in Ayurveda today were brought to India from China.

Both Ayurveda and TCM have a lot in common. They look at the human being as a whole and not just the disease. Both talk about the imbalance in the body and swear by the body's ability to heal. These also believe in the commonalities between the macrocosm (the universe) and the microcosm (the individual's body) and the healer's role as the conveyer belt between the macrocosm and the microcosm. This explains the similarities in the use of plant and animal extracts. Finally, both systems of thought focus on prevention as much as cure.

Both Ayurveda and TCM face similar problems while reaching out to the Western world. So it's high time they collaborate—in research, in collating/sharing knowledge and plugging gaps in knowledge. The two can together achieve a level of clarity and progress that neither is capable of, individually.

The big question is whether political differences between India and China will prevent such collaboration from becoming sustainable and long-lasting.

A Final Word

Concepts of Ayurveda are holistic. Ayurveda has leveraged the power of nature to help prevent illness and promote health. It trusts itself as much as it trusts the wonderful design of the human body. That partially explains Ayurveda's bold assertion that it can restore balance inside the human body and, indeed, restore the human body to its state of pristine glory.

The world needs Ayurveda and Ayurveda needs to bolster its attempts to reach out to the world. I'm tempted to say that, like with global climate change, the time to demand evidence is long over. There is more than enough evidence and we must act now to prevent a catastrophe.

Champions of Ayurveda must emulate the sense of urgency exhibited by global climate-change activists. But they should also be ready to work hard to convince the world that Ayurveda stems from solid science. Empirical evidence must become documented evidence. Documented evidence must become irrefutable proof. That's the only way to eliminate barriers to the practice of Ayurveda.

Here, Ayurveda can draw inspiration from itself—more specifically, its ability to integrate and adapt to emerging realities. For millennia, Ayurveda has eagerly integrated viable innovations, no matter where they have originated. It needs to do the same with the opportunities presented by modern science.

Needless to say, India must lead the change in this. There is a dire need to exponentially increase monetary and cerebral investments made in Ayurveda. When we do that, we will finally be able to convert this ancient science into a beacon of hope for the future.

Section II

Case Studies

12

Psoriasis

History

We were approached by a twenty-five-year-old man with severe, pinkish and blackish discolouration of skin all over his body, with scaling of the skin on both arms and the distal part of legs and forehead. He experienced severe itching throughout his body.

He developed small lesions just over the scalp about five to six years ago, which gradually spread to the hands and the back. He had visited a dermatologist at the onset of the disease and was given oral medication that reduced the lesions. However, the lesions spread all over the body after he stopped the medicine. Being an IT professional who sometimes worked night shifts, he had irregular food-consumption patterns, which aggravated his condition.

The young man went into depression as his skin lesions had a very bad effect on his social and personal life. Not only that, he found it difficult to carry on routine activities such as wearing a shirt or trousers. His flaky skin would fall off wherever he sat or moved, and he could not resist the need to scratch because of the constant itchiness. Activities such as swimming proved to be embarrassing. These challenges made him feel awkward and low in the presence of others. He had to purchase clothes that covered his body lesions and was forced to avoid attending social events and going out with friends. This gradually inched him towards becoming a social outcast. Deeply worried about his condition, his parents brought him to me to infuse normalcy back into his life.

Personal Pathophysiology Profile

The initial personal profiling revealed:

Factor	Focal Points	Impact on Treatment Decisions
Dūṣyas, dhātus (structural units)	Rasa, rakta, māṁsa, medās and lasika were affected	Several dhātus were drawn together, creating a complex condition that had to be carefully dealt with.
Bhoomi deśa (location)	Marshy	Geography had aggravated kapha imbalance, leading to the aggravation of the scaling and itching of the skin. Kapha pacification was done as the initial step.
Rogi bala (strength)	High	The patient could withstand the major pañca karma procedures with high-efficacy medications and varied treatment protocols.
Kāla (season)	Winter	Season had triggered the vitiated doṣa, aggravating his symptoms in the cold season, and treatments were planned accordingly.

Anala (digestive fire)	Low	His digestion was weak and toxins easily accumulated in the body. His agni had to be set right.
Prakṛti (constitution)	Pitta–kapha	Rogaanusaara pañca karma treatments that would not affect his prakṛti, were planned.
Vaya (age)	Youth	Quick results could be expected with good response from patient.
Satva (mental strength)	High	He had strong will and patience to undergo major pañca karma procedures and diversified therapies and medications easily.
Satmya (way of life)	He was used to working the night shift	This contributed to the vitiation of doṣas and dhātus. Healthy lifestyle guidance was provided.
Āhāra (food)	South Indian, non-vegetarian food. Irregular food habits, rice, milk products	Non-vegetarian food was avoided; healthy dietary changes were advised.

Treatment

We took the allopathic diagnosis as the first step and enhanced the case history by Ayurveda pathophysiological profiling of the patient with the above-mentioned details.

A customized topical and systemic course of treatments was devised for balancing all the doṣas and dhātus as follows:

Name of the Treatment	Description of the Treatment	Impact on the Body
Pañca karma therapies were implemented as below:		
Snehapanayukta vamana	Intake of medicated ghee on empty stomach and later, therapeutically induced emesis	Helps bring the toxins/vitiated doṣas into the GIT by oleating the body. These could then be expelled through therapeutically inducing emesis. May also help the body absorb the medications more effectively.
Mrudu abhyanga with specific oils	Warm medicated oil used for full-body massage given without much pressure	Improves blood circulation of the body, helps in easy movement of the toxins into the GIT for easy expulsion from body. Also gives psychosomatic soothing effect balancing the doṣas.
Takradhara-shiro and kaya takradhara	Lukewarm medicated buttermilk poured synchronously on the head and body for a stipulated time	Improves blood circulation, reduces burning sensation and itching of the skin, balances impaired doṣas of the skin, removes deep-seated skin toxins and rejuvenates the skin. Medications used may help inhibit cell proliferation of the skin. Has anti-inflammatory, antioxidant benefits. Relieves stress by promoting deep relaxation.
Oral medication	Pitta and kaphahara (reducing) medications administered	Helps in balancing pitta and kapha.

Sadhyovirechana	Therapeutically induced purgation without snehapana	Helps in removing the toxins accumulated in the intestines and balances the vitiated pitta doṣa.
Yoga basti	Nourishing and cleansing enemas	Helps in detoxification and especially balancing the vāta. Also helps in lubricating and nourishing the dhātus.
Lepa	Warm herbal paste application	Soothes and heals the skin.

Special care was taken in choosing the topical and the oral medications.

The patient was discharged after twenty-one days. The itchiness and dryness of the skin reduced within the next five days. The skin's unctuousness was restored, with reduced peeling. The patient felt great relief as the blackish lesions started to diminish. Pinkish skin on his arms and legs began acquiring their original hue; his appetite improved.

He was treated as an outpatient with regular follow-ups. His skin regained the normal colour and texture of a healthy person. His parents were happy to see their son confident, enthusiastic and socializing. He married a girl who also works in the IT industry.

Some time later, stress at work caused a relapse. However, this time around, he needed only ten days of treatment as an outpatient and he recovered quickly. To avoid further relapses, he was guided with a suitable lifestyle and diet, and gradually medications were stopped. The couple continues to come here for regular visits but mostly as a preventive practice.

13

Irritable Bowel Syndrome

History

We were approached by a forty-five-year-old man suffering from frequent mucous stools, abdominal cramps, bloated abdomen, burning sensation in the abdomen and tiredness.

He was in the habit of eating spicy food. As he travelled frequently on work, he had to consume outside food often. This led to indigestion and a bloated abdomen. He had constipation and loose stools occasionally. He used homoeopathy medicines and felt better for a few months. Due to stress and frequent travelling, he developed mucous stools and abdominal cramps, and had to pass frequent stools after having food. He had mouth ulcers, flatulence, bloated feeling and chest burn, because of which he had disturbed sleep and was easily irritable.

He had hypercholesterolemia (high cholesterol) and was taking allopathic medicines for over five years.

Personal Pathophysiological Profile

The initial personal profiling revealed:

Factor	Focal Points	Impact on Treatment Decisions
Dūṣyas, dhātus (structural units)	Rasa, rakta and māṁsa were affected	Multiple dhātus were involved and necessary pacificatory methods planned.
Bhoomi deśa (location)	Sadharanadeśa (balanced)	He could respond to the treatment without complications.
Rogi bala (strength)	Medium	Could tolerate the medications and procedures.
Kāla (season)	Summer	Loose bowels were augmented due to the temperature; fatigue was higher. Pitta-pacificatory measures were planned and restoration of body fluids had to be maintained.
Anala (digestive fire)	Vishama (erratic hunger—sometimes good and sometimes no hunger at all)	Caused improper digestion, leading to aama formation and poor nourishment to the tissues. Suitable agni-restoration medications was administered.
Prakṛti (constitution)	Vāta–pitta	Prakṛti was kept in mind while administering the line of treatment.
Vaya (age)	Middle age	Pitta aggravation happens in middle age, and the increased stress level made matters worse. Hence pitta pacification was implemented.
Satva (mental strength)	Medium	A few counselling sessions were planned as his work stress level was high.
Sātmya (way of life)	Going to bed late at night and travelling	This also led to an increase of pitta and vāta doṣa and major rectification was necessary in his way of life.
Āhāra (food)	Irregular food habits; north Indian food	Wheat and other rich foods aggravated the symptoms. Suitable dietary changes were suggested.

Treatment

We took the allopathic diagnosis as the first step and enhanced the case history by Ayurveda pathophysiological profiling of the patient with the above details.

This allowed us to offer a customized treatment:

Name of the Treatment	**Description of the Treatment**	**Impact on the Body**
Deepana medicines	Digestion-enhancing medicines such as *hingu vachadi choorna*	Enhances the digestive fire.
Pachana medicines	Ginger, black pepper, etc., were administered	Helps in removing the toxins (aama) and aids in normal functioning of digestive fire.
Indukanthākāśayam	A classical herbal decoction given orally	Strengthens the digestive system.
Daadimadighṛta	Classical medicated ghee given orally	Helps in healing the intestinal mucosa.
Chageryaadighṛta	Classical medicated ghee given orally	Helps in restoring the intestinal mucosa.
Grahanyantakaghṛta	Classical medicated ghee given orally	Aids in proper formation of stools, healing the GIT and restoring the digestive fire.
Takrariṣṭa	Classical medicated fermented preparation given orally	Acts as an anti-inflammatory on the intestines and aids digestion with kapha–vāta vitiating actions.
Sarvanga abhyanga	Full-body massage	Relaxes the mind and the body, balances the doṣas to a certain extent.

Mrudhuvirechana	Mild purgation	Detoxes the body and balances the vāta and pitta.
Rasāyanas	Oral, lickable medicines	Improves immunity, stamina and vitality.

Once agni was restored to normalcy, he was put on rasāyanas. With follow-ups at the OPD after fifteen days, we had reduced all the symptoms. The oil, which was given to apply on his head, reduced stress and also addressed his acidity and irritability. Medicines were given to further rejuvenate his digestive system and maintain stability. He was recommended a strict diet that included boiled buttermilk; he was asked to avoid fermented food, maida products, leafy vegetables and reheated food. He was also advised to avoid travelling during his IBS episodes. As this is a stress- and lifestyle-induced disease, he was advised to refrain from causative factors.

He is currently living a stress-free, normal life with the help of minimum oral medication.

14

Spinal Cord Injury

History

The case was of a forty-four-year-old man complaining of weakness in his legs; he was unable to move both upper and lower limbs, unable to sit or stand and unable to hold objects; he had a persistent cough. He had no bowel and bladder control and needed use of a silicone catheter. He was bed-ridden.

Having been in an accident, he had sustained a head injury followed by neck pain, and was unable to move any limb after that. Even after he underwent C7 corpectomy and fusion surgery, the symptoms mentioned above persisted. He was told that there was little chance of getting back on his feet. Physiotherapy was to be continued with a few oral medications. The patient, his wife and his relatives were depressed by his situation. He heard of our centre through word of mouth and came to us with high expectations of recovery.

Personal Pathophysiological Profile

The initial personal profiling revealed:

Factor	Focal Points	Impact on Treatment Decisions
Dūṣyas, dhātus (structural units)	Rakta, māṁsa, asthi and majja were affected	Multiple dhātus were involved and diverse treatments had to be planned.
Bhoomi deśa (location)	Dry	Contributed to the aggravation of vāta in the body. Vāta-pacifying and *brumhana* therapies were adopted.
Rogi bala (strength)	Moderate	The patient could withstand the treatments and medications.
Kāla (season)	Summer	The patient could undergo the planned treatments easily and results were achieved without any complications.
Anala (digestive fire)	Low	He was prone to accumulation of toxins in the body and poor nourishment to the body tissues. Digestive fire had to be normalized with medications.
Prakṛti (constitution)	Kapha–vāta	As vāta doṣa was predominant in both prakṛti of rogi and roga, therapies and medications were planned appropriately for balancing them.
Vaya (age)	Middle age	The patient could withstand diverse treatment as planned.
Satva (mental strength)	Medium	The patient could cooperate well during therapies with the help of a few counselling sessions.

Sātmya (way of life)	Moderate physical activities, going to bed late at night on a regular basis	Lifestyle modification suitable to him was suggested.
Āhāra (food)	Non-vegetarian food, irregular food habits	Due to low agni, his food habits could easily lead to toxin accumulation in the body. Dietary modification was advised.

Treatment

We took the allopathic diagnosis as the first step and enhanced the case history by Ayurveda pathophysiological profiling of the patient with the above-mentioned details, and the systemic and topical therapies were tailor-made with the best medicines as follows:

Name of the Treatment	**Description of the Treatment**	**Impact on the Body**
Virechana	Therapeutic purgation	Helps in expelling the toxins from the body; thus helps the body absorb the medications more effectively.
Dhanyamladhara	Warm fermented medicated water poured on the body	Helps in combating the kapha and vāta doṣa and relieving stiffness of joints.
Sarvanga abhyanaga	Full-body massage	Improves blood circulation in the body, relieves muscle stiffness, improves the tone of muscles and strengthens ligaments, tendons and joints. Also induces good sleep, which reduces stress and relaxes the mind. Balances all the doṣas, especially vāta doṣa.

Pichu	Warm oil packs on the cervical and lumbar region	Strengthens the ligaments and tendons of the spine.
Choorna pinda sweda	Special type of fomentation using herbal powders	Acts as kapha vātahara, and initiates elimination of vitiated doṣas and malas through the skin as perspiration.
Kashaya dhara	Suitable medicated warm decoctions poured over the body	Might help in stimulating the bladder to maintain its tone and function.
Tendon and *marma* massage	Special massage technique used on the tendons and joints of the legs	Enhances the blood supply to the dhātus and nourishes. Tones the tendons and muscles, helps in restoring the vāta.
Pizhichil	Special type of pouring of warm medicated oil on the whole body	Helps in deep nourishment and lubrication of all the dhātus of the body and thereby rejuvenates them. Stimulates the neuromuscular systems.
Yoga basti (eight in number—three asthapana bastis and five anuvasana bastis)	Cleansing and nourishing enemas	Helps in detoxification and especially balancing vāta. Also helps in lubricating and nourishing the dhātus.
Patra pinda sweda	A special type of fomentation with fresh herbal leaves	May help by improving blood circulation to the affected part and relieving pain and stiffness of the muscles and joints. Improves the muscular tone through its vātahara property, gets rid of doṣa imbalance.
Nadisweda	Medicated steam given on the affected part.	Helps in relieving pain, improves local blood circulation and reduces swelling.

Nasya	Medicated oil drops administered through the nose	Cleanses the *srotas* (microchannel) of head and helps in rapidly helping the medicines reach the brain.
Shastika shali pinda sweda	Special treatment with medicated milk and rice bolus fomentation	Helps in fortifying the dhātus and recovering muscle tone, with reduced muscle spasticity.
Lepa	Warm herbal paste applied on a certain part	Helps in reducing swelling and pain.
Talam	Warm oil pack on the vertex of head	Reduces vāta.
Paadabhyanga	Special foot massage	Improves blood circulation, has psychosomatic relaxation and stimulates motor functions, which pacifies the vāta doṣa.

This was done along with monitored oral medications.

Following an integrative approach, the patient was also given regular physiotherapy and yoga sessions. He was also sent to the neurosurgeon twice for neuro-related oral medications and review. Whenever required, his blood investigations were done and appropriate treatment suggested.

The patient was discharged after four months of treatment, when he was able to gain sensation in both legs, could easily sit without taking support and stand with support; he could even take a few steps with the help of a walker. He also started eating normal food and could shave his beard himself.

Gradually, he developed good control over his bowel movement but bladder control took time. He went back home happily with his wife, having dispelled the nightmarish prospect of being bed-ridden for the rest of his life.

He came back for one month of treatment as follow up, where he was given a second course of various vātahara and bruṁhana therapies and oral medications. He went back this time walking with very minimal support from a walking stick; he had regained quite a lot of sensation in both lower limbs, although he had to slightly drag his left foot while walking. He was able to attend to his routine activities and resumed work, aspiring to take his business to greater heights.

15

Diabetic Ulcer

History

A seventy-year-old woman was brought to me by her daughter with a wound in the right foot and bluish discolouration of her second and third toes. She complained of severe pain and foul smell; she had started using a wheelchair. Doctors had advised amputation of her toes. She had been diagnosed with diabetes mellitus seventeen years ago and was on insulin. Her blood sugar levels were still high as she was not following the diet appropriately. She had also been diagnosed with hypertension and was being treated for the same.

She suffered from frequent constipation, reduced appetite and joint pain. She had been treated using Ayurvedic methods for a diabetic wound some seven to eight years ago.

Personal Pathophysiological Profile

The initial personal profiling revealed:

Factor	**Focal Points**	**Impact on Treatment Decisions**
Dūṣyas, dhātus (structural units)	Rasa, rakta, māṁsa, medās, *lasika* (lymphatics) were affected	Multiple dhātus were involved and treatment had to be planned carefully.
Bhoomi deśa (location)	*Sadarana* (balanced)	She could respond to the treatment without complications.
Rogi bala (strength)	High	The patient could withstand the procedures well.
Kāla (season)	Winter	Doṣa-aggravating symptoms had become more prominent in the cold season and treatments were planned accordingly.
Anala (digestive fire)	Low	This led to easy accumulation of toxins.
Prakṛti (constitution)	Pitta vāta	Medications were selected not to hamper the prakṛti.
Vaya (age)	Old age	Only mild medications and therapies had to be administered.
Satva (mental strength)	High	She cooperated well during the treatments and procedures.
Sātmya (way of life)	Irregular food habits, going to bed late at night	It led to an imbalance of doṣas and the hormones produced by the body.
Āhāra (food)	South Indian, non-vegetarian food	The diet prescribed during the treatments wouldn't be difficult to follow.

Treatment

We took the allopathic diagnosis as the first step and enhanced the case history by profiling the patient (which led to the personal profile above). This allowed us to offer customized treatment with more topical therapies and minimal oral medications.

Here is a list of treatments that were prescribed for her:

Name of the Treatment	Description of the Treatment	Impact on the Body
Pañca karma treatments were administered as described below.		
Dhanyamladhara	Medicated fermented warm water poured on the body	Reduces inflammation and pain in the body.
Vranaprakshalana	The wound washed with kaṣāyas (herbal decoctions)	Helps in removing dead tissue and aids in the formation of granulation tissue.
Vrana lepana	*Jathyaadi ghṛta* and *tankana* applied	Promotes the healing of wounds.
Ardhanga abhyanga	Massage of both legs	Helps in improving blood circulation in the lower limbs, which aids the healing process.
Mrudu abhyanga with Dhanvantarataila	Mild full-body massage	Improves blood circulation, eases the movement of toxins into the intestines. Relaxes the body and mind.
Pañca patra Kashaya (or Kaṣāya) dhara	Lukewarm medicated decoction poured on the body	Helps in improving blood circulation and reducing pain
Mātrā basti	Enema given with medicated oil	Nourishes dhātus and pacifies vāta.

Kashaya basti	Cleansing enema	Pacifies vāta and helps in cleansing the intestines.
Oral medication	Oral medications	Helps in improving immunity, reducing blood glucose.

The above treatments reduced the discolouration of the toes completely. Though the wound in her sole was healing, it was deep and taking a long time to do so. She found it difficult to walk, which led to reduced physical activity. That, in turn, increased her blood sugar levels.

Following an integrated approach, we sought the opinions of an endocrinologist and a plastic surgeon. She was already on insulin and the appropriate dose was fixed by the experts. Wound debridement and regular vinegar dressing were done once a day, along with other therapies simultaneously for a few days. Later on, we used only vranaprakshalana, lepa and lower limb massages, which enhanced the granulation of the wound. Gradually, it healed completely, leaving behind only mildly visible scar tissue.

Final Outcome

She was treated for four months. By then, the ulcer had completely healed and blood glucose levels had come under control. She was completely free of constipation. Her appetite and sleep improved. She was able to walk independently. Her fear of amputation had vanished and she was happy as she could avoid the pain of surgery and loss of a limb.

Glossary of Terms

Name in Ayurveda	**Description**
abhyaṅga	Manual manipulation technique, in which oil is applied over various parts of the body to get the desired effect. A part of daily regimen adopted for preservation and promotion of health. Includes massage over the head (shiro abhyaṅga), massage over feet (pāda abhyaṅga) and oiling of ears (karna purana).
ādāna	Period of time when moisture, unctuousness and strength of the body get depleted and absorbed by the environment by virtue of climate; includes six months of winter, spring and summer.
agni	• One of the five basic elements (pañca mahābhūtas) that make up all matter in the universe. • All factors responsible for digestion and metabolism/transformation. Of three classes: jaṭharāgni (digestive elements in the GIT), bhūtāgni (metabolic factors involved in the digestion and absorption of the pañca mahābhūtas) and dhātvagni (metabolic factors that convert ahara rasa—nutrients from food—into the seven dhatus).

	• Physiologically, the intensity of agni is influenced by doṣas and is of four types: viṣama (irregular, due to the dominance of vāta), tīkṣṇa (intense, due to the dominance of pitta), manda (depressed due to the dominance of kapha) and sama (normal, due to the balanced state of all three doṣas).
agnimāndya	Lack of digestive power.
āhāra	Any substance that is masticated and swallowed for the purpose of nutrition and energy.
ajīrṇa	Refers to indigestion.
ākāśa	• A free or open space (occupied by the other four elements in different proportions, and is also the vehicle of sound). • One of the five basic elements (pañca mahābhūtas) that make up all matter in the universe.
ama	• Raw, uncooked, unbaked, immature, unripe • May be associated with food or other physiological entities to mean incomplete transformation or metabolism causing a harmful effect on health.
aṁbu	Water; the watery element of the body.
amla	Sour; one among six rasas.
anūpa	Marshy lands.
apāna vāyu	One of the five sub-types of vāyu (vāta), situated in the pelvic region. Performs functions such as defecation, micturition, parturition, menstruation and ejaculation.
ārtava	One of the upadhātus of rasa dhātu. Indicative of either menstrual fluid or ovum. It is dominant of agni mahābhūta.
asthi dhātu	Fifth of the seven basic dhātus, the bone tissue whose function is to provide stability to the body. Predominant of pṛthvi and ākāśa mahābhūtas. Designative of bone tissue.
ati	Excessive or hyperactive.

ātmā	Soul or spirit; the principle of life and sensation, the individual self; the only conscious element in the human body.
auṣadha	Medicine or drug.
avalaṁbaka	One of the five sub-types of kapha that supports and sustains the heart and other sites of kapha.
avara satva	A person having poor mental tolerance/inferior mind. Unable to endure even mild pain. Associated with fear, grief, greed, confusion.
āyu	• Span of life • Continuous combination of satva (mind), atma (soul), sharira (body) and indriya (sense organs)
Ayurveda	The science and knowledge of life, which describes all substances of the universe in terms of their being beneficial, harmful, pleasant and/or unpleasant to life.
bala	Strength; energy required to perform daily activities. Individual's strength has been classified into three types: sahaja = hereditary; yuktija = strength achieved from exercise, food, rasayana, etc.; and kalājā = natural strength received during visarga kāla (varsha, sharad and hemanta ritus).
bāla	Childhood (from birth to sixteen years), when dhātus are immature, secondary sexual characters are not manifested. Delicate body with incomplete strength. Dominance of kapha dhātu.
bhrājaka pitta	One of the five sub-types of pitta, which acts after jatharagni, but before dhatvagni on the food and its metabolites. They are: parthiva, apya, taijasa, vayaviya and nabhasa. They act on the corresponding substrate based on pañca bhautika composition to make them homologous to that of the bodily constituents.
bodhaka kapha	One of the five sub-types of kapha that helps in the perception of taste.

bramhā muhūrta	Relating to Bramha, Creator or Supreme Spirit, or to sacred knowledge or study. Muhūrta refers to a particular period of the day. Brahmā muhūrta includes forty-eight minutes of auspicious period before sunrise. It's a relevant time for thinking of brahmā or to study.
bṛṁhaṇa	All procedures and treatments that increase body weight and strength. For the emaciated, weak and debilitated, and for those in convalescence from chronic illness such as malabsorption, tuberculosis and anaemia. The reverse of reduction. Uses a rich diet of tonics, herbs, rest and relaxed lifestyle. Food prepared with ghee, butter, sesame oil, milk, raw sugar and jaggery.
deha	The living body. Indicative of growth in the bodily tissues.
deśa	Habitat, the place or environment where a plant or animal naturally or normally lives and grows.
dharma	Righteousness, justice, duty, obligations, disposition, distinctive quality, religious observance, etc. One of the four purushartas (values or goals of life) according to Hindus. The actions of a person that provide him/her heaven and happiness are treated as dharma. The opposite of this is adharma.
dhātu	The seven major structural components that stabilize and sustain the body (rasa, rakta, māṃsa, medās, asthi, majjā and shukra). The previous dhātu nourishes the next in a sequential fashion. Each dhātu is of two forms: sthāyī (stable) and poṣaka (nourishing). Each dhātu undergoes a cyclical process of origin, maturation and degeneration.
dhātvāgni	Seven types of agnis responsible for the transformation of one dhātu into another. They are rasagni, raktagni, māṁsagni, medās, agni, asthyagni, majjagni and sukragni.
dīpana	Stimulating/promoting digestion to increase appetite.

doṣa	Principle constituents of the body responsible for homeostasis, when present in the state of equilibrium. Determine the psycho–physiological nature/ constitution of an individual. Capable of vitiating the different bodily tissues when they deviate from the state of equilibrium and can lead to diseases. These are of two classes: ārīrika (bodily): • Vāta, pitta and kapha • Mānasa (psychological): raja and tama
duḥkha	Unhappiness, sorrow, woe, grief, misery, pain, anguish, agony, affliction, wretchedness, suffering, trouble, hardship, adversity, infliction, trial, tribulation. Any action that gives pain to indriyas (sense organs) and atma due to perception of adharma/paapa karma.
dūṣya	Any bodily structure that gets vitiated by aggravated doṣas.
gandha	Refers to smell.
gaṇḍūṣa	Filling the mouth to its full capacity with liquid (medicinal decoctions/lukewarm water/medicinal oils) without allowing its movement.
garbhāshayaḥ	The uterus. The organ of the female reproductive system for containing and nourishing the embryo.
ghṛta	Ghee.
hima	Cold infusion—the squeezed and filtered liquid after steeping overnight; the powdered material mixed with cold water in the ratio of 1:6.
hīna	Diminished.
jarā	A stage indicating the ages above forty-five years, when degeneration begins.
jāṭharāgni	The agni that acts on the food in the gastrointestinal tract to digest it.
kāla	Time in general, the point or period when something occurs, proper time or occasion, time of death.

kāma	Enjoyment; object of desire, love or pleasure; the third mansion to achieve the goal of life.
kapha	A synonym for shleṣmā. One of the three bodily doṣas responsible for stability, unctuousness, lubrication, immunity and cohesion. This is predominant of pṛthvi and jala mahābhūtas. The attributes are: guru (heavy), manda (dull), hima (cold), snigdha (unctuous), shlakṣṇa (smooth), mṛtsna (soft) and sthira (stable). Major seats are thorax, throat, head, pancreas, joints, stomach, rasa, medās, nose and tongue. Types: avalaṃbaka, kledaka, bodhaka, shleṣaka, tarpaka.
karṇa	Ear.
kaṣāya	Herbal decoction.
kaṣāyaka	Astringent; one among the six rasas.
kaṭu rasatā	Pungent taste or taste of chilli, one of the six rasas
lājā	Obtained by roasting undried and unhusked paddy. Is light and easily digestible. Cures thirst, vomiting, diarrhoea, diabetes, obesity, cough and pitta aggravation.
lepaḥ	A method of treatment in which medicines are used topically in the form of paste or ointment.
madhura	Sweet; one among six rasas.
madhyam vaya	Middle age in the sixteen–sixty-year range. Characterized by strength, virility, quality of all dhātus having reached the normal limits with proper physical and mental strength, without degeneration in qualities of dhātus with the predominance of pitta dhātu.
madhyama satva	Medium psyche; can sustain themselves with partial or full support of others (counsellor, etc.). Able to withstand grief, fear, anger, confusion and conceit to some extent.
mahābhūta	The great elements; the five proto-elements ākāśa, vaayu, teja, jala and pṛthvi, which are the basic constituents of all substances.

majjā	The marrow.
mala	The waste products of the body formed during various stages of digestion and metabolism. A fundamental constituent of the human body along with doṣa and dhātu. Of two classes: āhāramala and dhātumala. Āhāramala include mūtra (urine) and purīṣa (faeces). Dhātumalas: Kapha from rasa, pitta from rakta, nose mucus and ear wax from the māṃsa, sveda (perspiration) from the medās, nails and hair from the asthi, rheum of the eye from the majjā.
māṃsa	Flesh. The third dhātu among seven, whose function is to provide a covering over the skeleton. Dominant of pṛthvi mahābhūta.
mānasika bhāva	Thoughts or factor, attributes related to manas.
maṇḍa	A method of rice preparation. One part rice and fourteen parts water added and cooked. Liquid portion called maṇḍa (rice gruel) facilitates evacuation of flatus, relieves thirst and weakness, improves digestion, and softens the metabolic pathways.
mandāgni	The state in which the action of agni is considerably depressed due to dominant influence of kapha.
medās	The fourth dhātu among seven of the body, whose function is to provide snehana. Dominant of jala and prthvi mahābhūtas. Designative of adipose tissue and other lipids in the body.
mūtra	One of the liquid forms of āhāra-mala. Urine. Carries away kleda (watery waste) from the body.
nāsā	Means nose.
nidrā	Sleep; when the mana (mind) and indriyas (sense organs) get exhausted, they withdraw themselves from the objects and the individual gets sleep. Caused by tamas, kapha, physical and mental exertion; adventitious, as a sequel to diseases and normally at night.

pācaka pitta	One of the five sub-types of pitta situated in between the stomach and large intestine. Due to dominance of agni mahābhūta, this pitta is devoid of liquidity. Divides the food into sāra (nutritive) and kiṭṭa (waste) portions. This also supports other sub-types of pitta.
phāṁṭa	A filtrate obtained by steeping soft and aromatic substances in boiled water; in liquid form.
pitta	One of the three bodily doṣas responsible for digestion and metabolism in the body. Situated especially in umbilicus, stomach, sweat, lymph, blood, watery fluids of the body, eye and skin. Predominant of agni mahābhūta. Its attributes are: sasneha (slightly unctuous), tīkṣṇa (sharp), uṣṇa (hot), laghu (light), visra (of pungent odour), sara (flowing) and drava (liquid). Of five types: pācaka, ālocaka, rañjaka, bhrājaka and sādhaka.
prajñāparādhaḥ	Prajna refers to knowledge, intellect. Aparadha means offence, transgression or fault. Volitional transgression; erroneous deeds done on account of the impairment of intellect, wisdom and memory.
prakopa	Aggravation of vitiated doṣas in their own seats. The second stage of kriyakāla.
Prakṛti	• The nature of an individual or a substance. • The physical and psychological features specific to an individual that are produced to the dominant doṣa prevailing at the time of conception. Classified as deha prakrti (physical) and manasa prakrti (psychological). Deha prakrti may be produced due to the dominance of a single doṣa, two doṣas or due to a combination of all the three.
prāṇa	• Vitality • Breath of life • Spirit • Life

prāṇa vāyu	One of the five sub-types of vāta (vāyu) that is seated in the head. Performs functions such as controlling the intellect, heart, sensory and motor organs and mind. Also regulates activities such as respiration, spitting, sneezing, belching and swallowing.
puruṣaḥ	• The soul. • The living body. • Male.
rāga	Attachment, affection or sympathy.
rajas	• One of the three qualities (satva, rajas and tamas) or constituents of everything in creation. • Initiation, mobility, activity. The quality of passion, one of the three properties of manas and conceived as the fundamental substratum of the universe.
rakta	Blood, the second among seven dhātus whose function is jīvana (to give life). Formed in yakṛt (liver) and plīhā (spleen) with the help of rañjaka pitta and rakta dhātvagni. Dominant in agni mahābhūta. Named so because of its rakta or red colour.
raktamokṣaṇa	Bloodletting: a procedure for therapeutically removing morbid doṣa/poisons with blood. Blood can be eliminated through scraping, application of horn or leech or venesection. It is practised in poisoned blood and blood-borne diseases in pitta-predominant diseases (bilious) and also in a few vāta (neurological) disorders.
rañjaka pitta	One of the five sub-types of pitta situated in yakṛt (liver) and plīhā. This transforms rasa into rakta (blood).
rasa	Taste; feeling perceived by rasanendriya (tongue) when the substance comes in contact with it; six in number; each rasa indicates the pattern of pharmacological activity of the substance.

rasa dhātu	The first dhātu among seven and dominated by jala. This is pumped out of hṛdaya (heart) and continuously circulates all over the body to nourish other tissues. It is of nine anjalis in quantity. Vyāna and samāna vāyu help in its circulation. Its major function is prīṇana (nourishing).
rasāyana	Rasa signifies tissues of the body, ayana suggest a measure or methodology to saturate or enrich or conduct a special benefit to the body. One which has the capacity to enrich the sapthadhatu of the body or the drugs possessing the qualities to saturate or replenish the tissues. Drug or food that has the capacity to delay ageing, improve longevity, provide immunity against the diseases, promote mental competence, increase vitality and lustre of the body.
ṛitucaryaa	Two months together is called a ritu. Season Ṛitucaryaa denotes the work or duties to be carried out during each ritu. Includes seasonal food intake, seasonal activities and seasonal cleansing processes (ritu anusara shodhana).
roga	Discomfort; pain; disease.
sādhaka pitta	One of the five sub-types of pitta seated in the heart. Helps one achieve the desired goal and is also responsible for intellect, talent and self-respect.
sadvṛtta	Good conduct/behaviour of a man/woman to lead a healthy life. Conduct that is good at the physical, verbal, mental, social and spiritual levels.
sahaja bala	Constitutional strength, innate immunity.
samāgni	The state in which the action of agni is normal due to a balanced state of all the three doṣas.
samāna vāyu	One of the five sub-types of vāta (vāyu) that is seated in proximity to agni (in between the stomach and large intestine). Performs functions such as receiving food, digestion of the food, division of the food into useful and waste portions, and propulsion of food.

saṁcaya	Accumulation of vitiated doṣas in their own seats. First stage of kriyākāla.
saṁskāra	Transformation or processing or value addition.
sāmya	State of equilibrium or balance.
saptadhātu	Seven structural elements of the body: rasa, rakta, māṁsa, medās, asthi, majjā and shukra.
sātmya	Agreeable to natural constitution, wholesome, suitability, habituation.
satva	• One of the three qualities (satva, rajas and tamas) or constituents of everything in creation • Mind, harmony, natural character, inborn disposition, conscious mind, being in existence Also means mental tolerance or stamina. This is a quality of the mind. Three types: pravara, avara and madyama satva. Those with the pravara satva (strong willpower) are basically health-oriented and follow rules and regulation of swasthavritta and hence remain healthy. Their pain-bearing capacity is excellent; usually they do not fall ill, and whenever they are sick, it is easy to cure them.
shabda	The finest and most subtle source of the ākāśa mahābhūta.
shārīra guṇa	Synonym of gurvadi gunas; properties of substances that relate to the body and used as therapeutics.
sharīraḥ	The body.
shīta	Coolness; cold; an attribute of Vāyu and kapha. One of the twenty gurvadi gunas; caused due to activated jala mahābhūta; denotes physiological and pharmacological coolness; manifested by a reduction in burning sensation and thirst. Facilitates stoppage of flow in channels such as styptic, reduces sweating, increases urine, pacifies pitta, and aggravates vāta.
shodhana	A pharmaceutical process of purification/detoxification/refining/imparting useful properties in the material.

shūka dhānya	Grains with awn; monocotyledons.
shukra dhātu	The seventh dhātu whose function is reproduction. Generally equated with semen; dominant of jala mahābhūta. Present in two forms: • Pervading the entire body • Fertilizing the ovum
smṛti	Memory/reminiscence/recollection. That which results from a particular conjunction between the soul and the mind and also from impression. According to Charaka, memory is nothing but the remembrance of the things directly perceived, heard (scriptures) or explained earlier.
snāna	Bath. Taking a bath is auspicious, enhances virility, longevity, strength, compactness and the immune system (oja). At the same time, cures tiredness and rids the body of sweat and impurities.
sneha	Oiliness, unctuousness, lubrication, moisture, oil.
snigdha	Slimy/unctuous/oily; one of the twenty gurvadi gunas; caused due to activated jala mahābhūta; denotes physiological and pharmacological sliminess; manifested by moistening of body parts, increased strength and lustre; pacifies vāta, increases kapha.
srotas	• Structural or functional channels meant for the transportation of dhātu undergoing transformation. • Appearance of a srotas is similar to the dhātu that it transports.
sthānasaṁshraya	The interaction between the doṣas and dūṣyas. Fourth stage of kriyakāla representing the prodromal phase of a disease.
svarasa	Extracted juice of a plant part.
swastha	• Healthy; 'swa' and 'stha'. 'Swa' means own, self; and 'stha' means stable, steady; thus 'swastha' denotes self-abiding, being in one's natural state/prakṛti. • One who enjoys normal health.

sveda	Sweat, perspiration. Mala of medās dhātu. Withholds kleda (watery portion) in the skin.
taila	Oil.
takra	Buttermilk made by adding 1/4 part water to madhita. Prepared by churning the curd and removing butter from it.
talam	Palm or sole. Anterior or flex or surface of the hand from wrist to finger or sole of the foot.
tama	One of the three qualities (satva, rajas and tamas) or constituents of everything in creation.
tarpaka kapha	One of the five sub-types of kapha situated in the head. Nourishes different sensory organs.
tīkṣṇāgni	• Excessive digestive power. • The state in which the action of agni is considerably intensified due to the dominant influence of pitta.
tikta	Bitter; one among the six rasas. Synonym of the medicinal plant parpata.
triguṇa	The three primary attributes of the universe and also the properties of manas: satva, rajas and tamas.
tvacā	Skin. One of the five sensory organs. Perceives the sense of touch.
udāna vāyu	One of the five sub-types of vāta (vāyu), seated in the thorax. Performs functions such as effort, strength and recollection required for the production of speech.
upanāha	Poultice; application of the poultice prepared by substances that are unctuous, heavy and hot in property. Helps to pacify the vitiated vāta.
uṣṇa	Heat/hotness; one of the twenty gurvadi gunas; caused due to activated agni mahābhūta; denotes physiological and pharmacological hotness; manifested by increased agni, improved appetite and digestion, increased motion in channels; pacifies vāta and kapha, increases pitta. It is an attribute of pitta.

uttarāyaṇa/ādāna kāla	Ascent of the sun or its northward movement. This movement reduces the moisture (soumya) from the earth and takes away strength from living beings. Shishira, vasantha and greeshsma ritu together constitute uttarayana, which brings about reduction of strength.
vamana	Therapeutic emesis.
vaya	Age; defined as the state of the body corresponding to the length of time, broadly divided into three stages—childhood, adulthood and old age.
vāyu or vāta	One of the three bodily doṣas predominant of vāyu and ākāśa mahābhūtas. A vital biological factor that performs functions such as sensory perceptions, all motor activities and higher mental activities. Of five sub-types: prāṇa, vyāna, udāna, samāna and apāna. The major sites of distribution of vāyu are large intestine, pelvis, the extremities, ears, bones and skin. The attributes are rūkṣa (dry), laghu (light), shīta (cold), khara (rough), sūkṣma (minute), cala (mobile).
vega	Derived from 'vij'. Means: to agitate, to make quickly. In the medical context—natural urges (for elimination), reflex and excitement. Usually understood as natural urges of the body, which call for urgent satisfaction. In Ayurvedic parlance, it denotes natural reflexes or urges, which are of two types: dharaniya (suppressible urges), such as greed, anger, etc., and adharaniya (non-suppressible urges) such as sneezing, sleep, etc.
vikṛta kāla	Unwholesome time—if it is having a contrary impact, excessive or deficient to that of the seasons.
vilepī	A rice gruel preparation differing in consistency from peya and more solid. To prepare vilepi, four parts of water and one part of broken rice are taken and boiled until the rice turns soft.

viruddha āhāra	Incompatible food—the food, drinks and medicine, which dislodges doṣa from its site, i.e. doṣotklesa, but does not expel it, and acts contradictory to the body tissues. They do not help in the nourishment of dhātu and, in due course, produce many diseases. Food which is an antagonist to the body and dhātu.
vīrya	• The principle responsible for the therapeutic action of the substance; comparable with the fraction of a substance containing the active principles; ascertained either by contact or duration of its stay in the body • One of the bases of nomenclature of plants
vīrya	• Strength, power, energy, efficacy • Semen
viṣamāgni	The state in which the action of agni is rendered erratic (either excessive or decreased, variable from time to time) due to the dominant influence of vāta.
vyāna vāyu	A sub-types of vāta that is seated in hṛdaya (heart). Responsible for pumping rasa from the heart to all parts of the body. It controls all types of movements in the body.
yavāgu	Gruel; a type of congenial preparation of cereals such as rice, wheat, barley, etc. Types: manda (only the liquid portion of the prepared gruel), peya and vilepi.
yūṣa	Soup prepared with pulses; a semi-solid preparation obtained by boiling any type of pulses but not rice. To prepare yusa as a liquid, kwata/swarasa/hima/takra and kalka of ousadha dravyas are taken and processed by adding water in the ratio of 1:16.

Treatment Glossary

Name	Description
avagāhana	Immersion of anointed body in a tub of warm water. A daily regimen that nourishes the whole body, bestows strength, gives stability and enhances physical resistance.
bhashpasweda	Sudation in a steam chamber.
choorna pinda sweda	Medicated powder fomentation.
deepna and paachana	Oral medicines that are digestive and carminative.
dhanyamaladhara	Special, medicated and fermented water massage. Warm, fermented medicated water poured on the body.
ishtika sweda	A type of fomentation treatment using hot brick and medicated concoctions/fermented liquids applied on the heels useful in calcaneal spur.
jihwa lepa	Herbal application on the tongue.
kaṣāyadhara	Medicated concoction synchronously poured in a thin stream on the body.

ksheeradhooma	Medicated milk fomentation.
lepa	Medicated paste application.
marma massage	A unique body massage concentrating on vital points of the body.
mātrā basti	Nourishing enemas using suitable medicated oil/ghee.
nasya	Instilling/slow pouring of medicated oil into the nose.
padabhyanga	Foot massage.
patra pinda sweda	Sudation with fresh medicated herbs.
pichu	Warm oil packs applied on a part of the body.
pizhichil like abhyanga	A special type of oil massage.
prusta	Vertebral column, lower back and buttocks.
samāṁsa shastika shali pinda	Shastika shali pinda sweda using meat as an added ingredient.
sarvanga abhyanga	Full body massage with suitable medicated oil.
shastika shali pinda sweda	Unique hot fomentation massage for rejuvenation purpose. Treatment with medicated milk and rice bolus fomentation.
shirothalam	Oil pack applications on the head.
takra dhara	Systematic and regulated pouring of medicated buttermilk on head/body in lying position for forty-five to sixty minutes for a period of one, three or seven days. It is commonly used for the treatment of chronic skin diseases, mental disorders, sleeplessness, and scalp and hair disorders.
talam	Oil packs on the vertex of head.
tendon massage	Unique massage concentrating on the tendons of the body. A Marma technique.

thalapothichil	Specific herbal paste applied on the head and covered with herbal leaves for a stipulated period.
upanaha	Warm poultice applied on the affected joints.
virechana	Therapeutically induced purgation.
yoga basti	A combination of suitable medicated oil and decoctions, enemas, which are nourishing and cleansing in action.

Acknowledgements

I bow to Lord Dhanvantari for making me capable enough to do this work.

I am grateful to Padmabhushan professor Dr M.S. Valiathan, for providing an exhaustive foreword to this book.

I thankfully remember Professor Bhushan Patwardhan, former vice chairman of the University Grants Commission; Vaidya Rajesh Kotecha, secretary of the Ministry of AYUSH, Government of India; and Vaidya Jayant Deopujari, chairperson of the board of governors, Central Council of Indian Medicine (CCIM), Government of India, for their kind appreciation of my work.

I am thankful to Dr Sriranjini Jaideep, PhD, NIMHANS, for going through the first draft of the manuscript and providing useful inputs; Dr Shalini T.V., MD (Ayurveda); Dr Kusuma T.V., MD (Ayurveda); and Dr Pushya A. Gautama, MD (Ayurveda), for stepping in at different points during the progression of manuscript and adding their valuable inputs and research data.

I am grateful to B.N. Subramanya, a dear friend and an adviser to the chairman, Gokula Education Foundation, who was instrumental in me taking this project up.

I am also thankful to Sujatha Kelkar Shetty, for encouraging me to write this book and helping me find a good publisher.

I place on record my sincere appreciation of Dr M.K. Vivek Sanker, MD, PhD, for giving his useful comments after going through the manuscript.

I bow to my father, Sri K. Gopinathan Nair, who is 102 years old, a veteran of the Indian naval force, whose healthy presence at all times has been an extraordinary energizing factor for me.

Thanks are also due to my secretary, Narayan Prakash, and former secretary, Ranganath Prasad, for meticulously going through the manuscript word by word and making corrections wherever necessary.

My profound thanks to my caring and supportive wife, Dr T.K. Girijakumari, MD, MBA (Hospital Management) and PhD, who always stands with me; and my children Ganapathy, Gopinath and Gopika, for their support and for going through the manuscript whenever I wanted them to.

I am indebted to my sisters, Srimati G.G. Geetha, a Sanskrit scholar, for handholding me in the world of the Sanskrit language and literature during my formative years, and Gayathri; Sasidharan, my brother-in-law; Dr B.G. Gokulan, a well-known Ayurveda ophthalmologist and founder of the Sudharshanam Netra Chikithsalayam, Tiruvalla, Kerala, and his wife Shanthi Gokul, for their support. Thanks to my artist brother Giridharan Nair, a saintly person, who has been a constant listener whenever I wanted to discuss things, and his wife Usha.

And to my mother, late C.K. Bhargavi Amma, who has been guiding me since my childhood to the very last days of her physical existence. I am sure she is watching us from heaven and I feel her presence every day.

Last but not the least, my pranam to my spiritual guru and mentor, late Sri P.R. Krishnakumar-ji, for introducing me to the wonderful world of Ayurveda through his innovative seven-and-a-half-year Ayurvedacharya course at a gurukula platform started by him in 1975 in the sylvan background of Western Ghats bordering Coimbatore.

I hope to be forgiven if I have left out any names who have helped me at different points, directly or indirectly.